"Colberg masterfully deconstructs the widely held assumption that the Second Vatican Council turned its back on the First Vatican Council. By asking 'what,' 'how,' and 'why' they taught about issues of authority, infallibility, and collegiality, she reveals the common concerns and shared commitments of these two very different ecclesial events. The result is a compelling chapter in the story of a living tradition—a century-long struggle to discover what it means to be church in the modern world. This is an invaluable contribution to the ongoing reception of both Vatican councils."

— Edward P. Hahnenberg, PhD, author of *A Concise Guide to the Documents of Vatican II*

Aug 2   Preface & Chapter 1
Aug 9   Chapter 2 & 3
Aug 2316 Chapter 4 & 5
Aug 23   Chapter 6
Aug 30   Chapter 7

VATICAN I
AND
VATICAN II

Councils in the Living Tradition

Kristin M. Colberg

A Michael Glazier Book

LITURGICAL PRESS
Collegeville, Minnesota

www.litpress.org

A Michael Glazier Book published by Liturgical Press

Cover design by Jodi Hendrickson.

Library of Congress Cataloging-in-Publication Data

Names: Colberg, Kristin, author.
Title: Vatican I and Vatican II : councils in the living tradition / Kristin M. Colberg.
Description: Collegeville, Minnesota : Liturgical Press, 2016. | "A Michael Glazier book."
Identifiers: LCCN 2015047503 (print) | LCCN 2016005269 (ebook) | ISBN 9780814683149 (pbk.) | ISBN 9780814683392 (ebook)
Subjects: LCSH: Councils and synods—History. | Catholic Church—History—19th century. | Catholic Church—History—20th century. | Vatican Council (1st : 1869–1870 : Basilica di San Pietro in Vaticano) | Vatican Council (2nd : 1962–1965 : Basilica di San Pietro in Vaticano)
Classification: LCC BX825 .C54 2016 (print) | LCC BX825 (ebook) | DDC 262/.52—dc23
LC record available at http://lccn.loc.gov/2015047503

Contents

Preface

Why Examine The Relationship between Vatican I and Vatican II?

For many Catholics as well as for non-Catholics, the relationship between the First Vatican Council (1869–1870) and the Second Vatican Council (1962–1965) is marked either by ambiguity or, worse, by opposition. For many, the name Vatican I immediately prompts the words "papal infallibility," "centralized authority," and "clerical leadership," while the name Vatican II sets off the words "college of bishops," "local church," and "lay leadership." These spontaneous associations of words usually imply either that these two assemblies are disconnected from each other or that they oppose each other in their ecclesiological visions. When taking the latter perspective, Catholics often feel pressed to identify themselves as proponents either of Vatican I or of Vatican II—but not of both. Can such a view be correct?

This was my question when as a graduate student I selected Vatican I as the subject of a major research paper. At the time, my knowledge of the council was exhausted by two basic pieces of information: (1) it defined papal infallibility and (2) many people had a negative view of its decrees. Even with minimal knowledge of Vatican I, I already possessed a nascent impression that the council was misguided, outdated, and relatively unimportant. My professor was at a loss as to why, given the vast possibilities in the field of ecclesiology, I would devote significant time to what he assumed would be another dry paper on papal infallibility. My motivation was not, however, a desire to investigate the finer points of the pope's power; rather I wanted to know *"what was Vatican I trying to do?"* Presuming that Vatican I presented an inappropriate notion of authority and an inadequate view of freedom,

I wanted to appreciate the council's intent in the hope of understanding its teachings in new ways. Knowing that Vatican I and its presentation of authority presents a major stumbling block for many contemporary men and women, it seemed essential to offer some account of papal infallibility that was not entirely incompatible with modern notions of freedom. My investigation initially arose from questions about the church's ability to speak meaningfully in the modern context and a sense that, while perhaps flawed, its teachings on authority need not be seen as opposed to modern men's and women's sense of themselves and experience of the world.

Over time, this project became a study not just about Vatican I but also about Vatican II and the relationship between them. This expanded focus was organic. In examining what Vatican I was trying to achieve, it became clear that *Vatican I shared many of the same concerns and intentions as Vatican II*. This insight stands at the heart of this study. Recognizing critical aspects of continuity between these councils provides both immediate and proximate benefits. In an immediate sense it contributes to a more adequate reading of each council while offering a perspective for interpreting their relationship. The relationship between Vatican I and Vatican II remains largely unexplored as a resource for Catholic theology. This lacuna is particularly notable when one considers that current debates over Vatican II's interpretation center on the nature of its relation to tradition—specifically the question of the extent to which it reflects continuity and/or rupture with its conciliar predecessors. The void in theological reflection on the relationship between Vatican I and Vatican II can be attributed, to a large extent, to the fact that the teachings of these two councils and, significantly, their intentions, are widely presupposed to be incompatible. This perception is fueled, largely, by inadequate interpretations of Vatican I. This book seeks to provide a properly contextualized reading of Vatican I's presentation of papal authority in order to better understand its teachings and bring its voice into the conversation about Vatican II's interpretation. Rehabilitating Vatican I exerts something of a domino effect. Appreciating the meaning of Vatican I's definition of papal infallibility in its appropriate setting illumines the importance of the questions it raised and the consequence of the incomplete answers it produced. This enhanced reading of Vatican I offers deeper appreciation of Vatican II questions which, in turn, facilitates a greater awareness of the significance and character of the conversations that have followed it.

In a broader sense, studying the relationship between Vatican I and Vatican II provides insight into overarching theological concerns, including the hermeneutics of conciliar interpretation, the nature of the church's tradition, the character of the church-world relationship, and the effective proclamation of the Gospel. This book, therefore, examines the relationship of Vatican I and Vatican II as an important theological locus in its own right and as a window into fundamental theological concerns. A key principle of dogmatic hermeneutics is that conciliar teachings must be read in light of the entire tradition and from the perspective of the way in which such discrete teachings can be integrated within that whole. Evidence of the importance and prominence of this principle can be found throughout the conciliar tradition, including within the documents of Vatican I, which take pains to show their positions as rooted in and building on the work of the council's predecessors. Seeing councils within this larger framework reflects a principle at the heart of the Christian tradition, namely, that conciliar teachings exist as part of a living tradition. They do not intend to be the only word on a particular topic; rather, they define a valid presentation of an issue that can and must be held in tension with other valid presentations. Isolating or polarizing particular councils contradicts this hermeneutical principle and raises serious theological problems.

That conciliar decrees must be seen against the expansive backdrop of the Christian faith understood holistically means that the church must engage in continual re-readings and re-receptions of them. The church must move beyond the sense that the acts of re-reading and contextualizing call into question the legitimacy of the church's tradition or its ability to adequately interpret its own positions. Efforts at re-reading need not suggest a failure of original readings and receptions. On the contrary, it is a sign of ecclesial vitality and a community that witnesses to a living tradition. An active and ongoing reception of doctrine resists stacking

Christian teachings one on top of the other as if they were inanimate; it rather integrates the content of sacred tradition into the life of the faithful through the spirit of Christ who makes all things new. The need for continual re-readings and re-receptions suggests that conciliar texts are never finished. Their teachings can always be better understood by refracting their meaning through the lens of other legitimate expressions of the faith.

This book provides a coherent account of the relationship between the First Vatican Council and the Second Vatican Council. It argues that Vatican I and Vatican II do not stand in opposition to one another but enjoy a relationship of complementarity. In other words, their relationship is not one of *either/or* but one of *both/and*. Drawing on the church's own tradition as well as the best of historical and theological scholarship concerning Vatican I and Vatican II, the chapters that follow demonstrate that properly contextualizing these councils illumines fundamental agreement between them; an agreement that is sufficiently strong to allow their difference to be seen as complementary rather than mutually exclusive. In order to express the full catholicity of the Catholic faith and present it effectively in the modern context, the church must develop lenses for interpreting its tradition that can fruitfully integrate all legitimate aspects of it.

The book's account of the both/and relationship between Vatican I and Vatican II unfolds in eight chapters. The first chapter considers the nature of the church's conciliar tradition and the problems that arise from attempts to polarize particular councils and, in particular, the two most recent councils. It argues that efforts to set Vatican I and Vatican II in a competitive relationship, usually as a means of achieving clarity, frustrate the church's ability to present a coherent message and speak meaningfully today. Chapter 2 establishes the context in which Vatican I's decrees can be read appropriately; specifically, it looks at historical and theological factors which influenced *why* Vatican I taught what it taught. Chapter 3 engages in a close reading of Vatican I's definition of papal infallibility by attending to the way that the council's context influenced both the form and the content of this teaching. It demonstrates that (1) *what* the council taught is considerably more limited than is generally perceived and (2) *how* the council taught is considerably less rigid. Chapter 4 examines the immediate reception of Vatican I's teaching on papal infallibility following the council's suspension. In particular, it considers how the council's inability to complete the more comprehensive document on the church it had intended impacted the way that some bishops interpreted the meaning of its texts.

Attention shifts in chapter 5 to the historical and theological context of Vatican II. It demonstrates that the teachings and silences of Vatican I serve as a critical context for the drama and decisions that unfolded at Vatican II. In other words, a significant element of *why* Vatican II taught what it taught was the need to balance and complete Vatican I's texts. The sixth chapter examines *what* and *how* Vatican II taught regarding the authority of the bishops in *Lumen Gentium* 18–23. This examination highlights how the content and style of Vatican II's presentation of episcopal authority draws from Vatican I's presentation of papal authority in key ways. The final chapter explores the *both/and* character of the relationship between Vatican I and Vatican II. The chapter illustrates that proper contextualization of both councils illumines fundamental continuity between their presentations of the church. It sketches some of the vast implications of this relationship for the church's engagement with a wide range of contemporary issues and its efforts to advance critical dialogues.

This book is about the relationship between Vatican I and II and what this relationship reveals regarding the nature of the church. It retrieves Vatican I from the margins of Catholic discourse and, in doing so, initiates a chain reaction, the end result of which is a greater ecclesial self-understanding and more coherent Christian discourse. The contextualization achieved by directing questions of *why*, *how*, and *what* at each council demonstrates that Vatican I and Vatican II are fundamentally harmonious, offering a coherent presentation of many issues on which the church is often charged with incoherence. Providing a more accurate view of this relationship succeeds in the original aim of asserting the church's ability to speak meaningfully in the modern context and to provide satisfying answers to the questions posed by modern men and women. It facilitates the church's efforts to speak meaningfully by affirming the coherence of the church's presentation of topics such as authority and freedom and by clarifying the character of the church's living tradition.

Before proceeding, I would like to acknowledge many of the people who have assisted in bringing this book to publication. My greatest debt is owed to Robert Krieg of the University of Notre Dame and to Shawn Colberg of the College of Saint Benedict and Saint John's University. Bob has been a constant source of support, ideas, editorial assistance, and friendship. He has spent countless hours discussing this manuscript with me and has read drafts of it at every stage. No one could ask for a better or more dedicated mentor. His generosity of time with his students and colleagues, skill in teaching, outstanding scholarship, clarity in writing, and sense of humor are things that I hope to emulate in my own career. Shawn has been a partner in this project, and without him it would not exist. Everything that I have written is better for having discussed it with him, from having learned from him, and from his superb editing of my work. He also acted selflessly to create the time and space needed for research and writing. I could never express the full extent of my gratitude for all Shawn did so that my goals could be realized.

Many others have played invaluable roles in the development of this book. Mary Catherine Hilkert has been an outstanding teacher and friend; she has been a constant source of support and provided critical feedback that shaped the overall argument of this project. Cyril O'Regan has been a major influence on my development as a scholar and remains a great friend. From the beginning he saw the value of this project and worked consistently with me to broaden the scope of my theological inquiry and sharpen my research methods. John Cavadini has also been a tremendous source of assistance and a role model. He provides an example of what it looks like to engage in important scholarly work done in service of the church. J. Matthew Ashley encouraged me through every stage of writing and helped me to think about ways to balance writing with other areas of my life and work. Hermann Pottmeyer generously read a draft of this manuscript and provided crucial feedback. Finally, conversations over the course of several years with Cardinal Walter Kasper have also proven invaluable.

I would also like to thank the Department of Theology at the College of Saint Benedict and Saint John's University and the School of Theology at Saint John's University for the support they provided during the writing of this manuscript. Thanks also go to my colleagues on the Reformed-Catholic dialogue who helped me to think about the ecumenical implications of this study. Additionally, I am grateful to Liturgical Press and Hans Christoffersen, in particular, for their superb handling of this project through the many stages of its publication.

Heartfelt gratitude goes to my family, particularly my daughters Mary Clare and Catherine. They are a source of constant joy and pride. They remained good natured and positive all the times when mom had to "go to work." When I would feel frustrated and not sure about how to move forward Mary Clare would say, "Mom, if you don't know what to say just write, 'violence doesn't solve anything.'" So, I add her contribution here. To be equitable, Catherine's suggestion was "always do your best." Thanks also goes to my father, Gene Brantman, who passed away in the course of this project but who would have been among the first to help me celebrate its conclusion. My mother, Kathleen Bell, and stepfather, Dennis Bell, have been incredibly supportive throughout the many stages of this book's development; their generosity in many things helped make this project a reality. I am also grateful to my sister Ally, brother-in-law Mario, nephew Mario, and niece Lulu and to my in-laws, Mike and Karin Colberg, for their help and the respite they provided along the way. Several other teachers, friends, and colleagues contributed to this project in invaluable ways, including Lawrence Cunningham, Richard McBrien, Lamen Sanneh, Randall Zachman, Margaret Farley, Edward Hahnenberg, Christopher Ruddy, Harold Ernst, Rita George Tvrtković, Steve Rodenborn, Elizabeth Miller, Colleen Hogan Shean, and Jennifer Deslongchamps. This book would not be possible without the friendship and support of these people. The joy of this publication stems not only from its content but in recognizing a deep and life-giving network of friends and colleagues who have made the goals I set for myself possible.

CHAPTER ONE

Vatican I and Vatican II as Part of a Living Tradition

The central hermeneutic problem in the reception of Vatican II is: Is Vatican II to be read in the light of Vatican I, or is the direct opposite the case, or will the as yet unachieved reconciliation of the two councils show the necessity of a further stage in the development of ecclesial self-understanding?[1]

—Hermann Pottmeyer

The First Vatican Council began on December 8, 1869, in Rome's St. Peter's Basilica, and it abruptly adjourned on October 20, 1870, in this same grand church. It was comprised of approximately 737 participants. These bishops and church officials, most of whom were from Europe, set out to work on fifty-one schemas or proposed decrees. They managed, however, to discuss only six of these texts, of which they acted on only two. To be precise, they approved only one part of one text and one part of another text. They departed from St. Peter's Basilica after eleven months following the outbreak of the Franco-Prussian War.

---

[1] Hermann Pottmeyer, "A New Phase in the Reception of Vatican II: Twenty Years of Interpretation of the Council," in *The Reception of Vatican II*, ed. Giuseppe Alberigo, Jean-Pierre Jossua, and Joseph A. Komonchak, trans. Mathew J. O'Connell (Washington, DC: The Catholic University of America Press, 1987), 27–43, at 33.

The Second Vatican Council commenced on October 11, 1962, also in Rome's St. Peter's Basilica, and it ended there on December 8, 1965. The council included more than 2,600 bishops from all around the world, who sat in bleacher-like rows of seats that ran the length of the church's nave. These bishops and church officials initially received seven draft texts or schemata for their deliberations, and yet after their four sessions they generated sixteen documents, of which four are "constitutions," nine are "decrees," and three are "declarations."

Although these two councils are separated by less than a hundred years, they can seem to stand apart in many ways. In the five decades that have passed since Vatican II's conclusion, there is still no consensus regarding its relationship with its predecessor. It seems that for many scholars, the only link between these councils is geography, or at best, their nomination in the official canon of ecumenical councils. The question thus arises: what is the relationship between these two significant church assemblies? While this question is important in itself, it also surfaces other questions about what came after these councils and the nature of the church itself. In the decades since Vatican II, and particularly within the last twenty-five years, the church has focused increased attention on the theme of reception and shifted to greater governance through regional synods. Some argue that the increased reliance on gathering the bishops in this manner is inconsistent with, or even a rejection of, the notion of papal authority offered by Vatican I. Others assert that the increasing use of synods indicates that Vatican II's teachings have become outdated, and the church has moved beyond them. In light of these conflicting perceptions, one must ask: what does the current shape of the church have to do with either of these councils? While the connections between these developments are not always understood or appreciated, there are critical links between Vatican I and Vatican II and the models emerging in the church today. Recognizing continuity between these councils is essential for understanding them and, more broadly, for appreciating the nature of the church's living tradition.

A critical problem today is that many people are unwilling to acknowledge any continuity or positive relationship between Vatican I and Vatican II. They see these councils as offering conflicting positions on fundamental themes such as the character of the church-world relationship, the nature of revelation, and the exercise of ecclesial authority. These differences seem to suggest that Vatican I and Vatican II are incompatible and therefore, rather than studying them together, one is forced to decide between them.[2] This creates the perception that one must choose *either* Vatican I's presentation of the church *or* Vatican II's. Presented with such a dichotomy, it is generally the case that Vatican II's teachings are preferred to those of its predecessor.[3] Vatican I's tone, its centralized view of the church, and its definition of papal infallibility appear to be at odds with contemporary sensibilities and, as such, are elements that many are eager to leave behind. Thus, for some, allowing Vatican I to recede into the distance seems to provide the best solution; it allows dialogue to proceed more quickly by avoiding the lengthy detour of engaging Vatican I's teachings more carefully and locating them within the larger Catholic tradition. There are others in the church, however, who resent Vatican II for seemingly disrupting the longstanding certainties of Catholicism. These Catholics would like to see Vatican II recede into the past as the hierarchy rebuilds the church and restores its strong foundation.

The solution of polarizing Vatican I and Vatican II which, on one level, appears to solve seemingly intransigent challenges, in fact, creates critical problems. Setting the teachings of these councils as oppositional contributes to the perception of the church's incoherence on multiple levels. On one level, it frustrates the

---

[2] At present there are no monograph-length scholarly studies that consider Vatican I and Vatican II in relation to one another. In recent years, however, increased attention has been directed at exploring the relationship between Vatican II and the Council of Trent (1545–1563). An excellent volume comparing the two councils is *From Trent to Vatican II: Historical and Theological Investigations*, ed. Raymond Bulman and Frederick Parrella (London: Oxford University Press, 2006). While such studies have borne considerable fruit, it is notable that their success has not yet inspired scholars to produce similar comparisons between Vatican II and its immediate predecessor.

[3] Regarding contemporary preferences for Vatican II over Vatican I, a telling anecdote is that when one attempts a Google search of "Vatican I history" the first result which appears is "Did you mean 'Vatican II history'?"

interpretation of Vatican I's and Vatican II's texts by failing to recognize the existence of significant continuity and complementarity between them. The councils convened by Pius IX and John XXIII met roughly one hundred years apart and include the only two constitutions on the church in the conciliar tradition. Reading their presentations of the church together allows them to reflect light on one another, which illumines elements of their meaning that cannot be seen when the councils are viewed in separate silos of interpretation.

On a more global scale, the denial of a dynamic relationship between Vatican I and Vatican II conflicts with critical aspects of the church's self-understanding. Fundamental to Christian theology as a whole and the conciliar tradition in particular is the belief that the Holy Spirit guides the church in formulating its teachings and cannot contradict itself. Accordingly, the Christian paradigm maintains that all expressions of divine revelation legitimately established in the church's tradition norm one another and work together to convey aspects of the one Christian faith. As such, conciliar teachings exist as part of a living tradition; they do not intend to be the only word on a particular topic but a valid presentation of a matter of faith to be held in tension with other valid presentations. This point is expressed by Cardinal Walter Kasper who notes that:

> An important concept, valid for all Councils [is that] the church is the same in all centuries and in all Councils. That is why each council is to be interpreted in the light of the whole tradition and of all Councils. The Holy Spirit who guides the church, particularly its Councils cannot contradict Himself. What was true in the first millennium cannot be untrue in the second. Therefore the older tradition should not be simply considered as the first phase of a further development. The other way around is also true: the later developments should be interpreted in the light of the wider, older tradition.[4]

---

[4] Walter Kasper, "Introduction to the Theme and Catholic Hermeneutics of the Dogmas of the First Vatican Council," in *The Petrine Ministry: Catholics and Orthodox in Dialogue*, ed. Walter Kasper (Mahwah, NJ: Newman Press, 2006), 7–23, at 17.

Giuseppe Alberigo provides a helpful image for conveying this point by observing that the great conciliar assemblies constitute the "spinal column" of the Christian tradition. He adds that "knowledge of their unfolding offers the church an awareness of its basic choral dimensions and evidence of crucial instances of the Spirit's interventions in history."[5] Similar to the way that a chorus derives its beauty not in monotony but in a mix of voices that provide points and counterpoints, the conciliar tradition requires a variety of expressions, held in tension with one another, to illumine the mystery at the heart of the Christian faith. Attempting to polarize the teachings of Vatican I and Vatican II not only threatens a kind of choreographic richness in their ongoing interpretations but also leads to something of a "conciliar scoliosis" or unnatural curvature of interpretation which threatens to miss the Spirit's full disclosure to the people of God.

The principle that each council must be seen in the context of the whole conciliar tradition has not always been observed in efforts to interpret Vatican I and Vatican II. Not enough has been done to consider how Vatican I's teachings, with their seemingly sharp edges, might be better understood and tempered when placed in a wider theological context. Instead, Vatican I's teachings, particularly its definition of papal infallibility, are regularly isolated from other legitimate teachings of the theological tradition—thus obfuscating their meaning. Similarly, trying to understand Vatican II properly, in the context of the whole Christian tradition, cannot be achieved if its immediate predecessor is eschewed and Vatican II is placed into a tradition that ignores that which directly preceded it. In recent years, considerable attention has been given to Vatican II's relationship with the larger conciliar tradition and, in particular, to the question of whether Vatican II represents rupture or continuity with the rest of the conciliar tradition.[6] Strikingly, Vatican I's voice is rarely introduced into the

---

[5] Giuseppe Alberigo, preface to *History of Vatican II*, vol. 1: *Announcing and Preparing Vatican Council II*, ed. Joseph A. Komonchak and Giuseppe Alberigo (Maryknoll, NY: Orbis Books; Leuven: Peeters, 1995), xi–xv, at xi.

[6] A good summary of some of the central aspects of this debate and its implications is found in Neil Ormerod, "Vatican II—Continuity or Discontinuity?

conversation.[7] Given Vatican I's and Vatican II's chronological proximity and shared focus on the church, the question of Vatican II's relation to tradition ought not to be adjudicated apart from considering the ways that it can be seen as continuous and discontinuous with its most immediate predecessor. To fully understand Vatican I and Vatican II, they must be subject to the normal and common principles of dogmatic hermeneutics which demand that they be viewed in relation to one another and within the conciliar tradition as a whole.

Finding harmony between Vatican I's and Vatican II's positions requires re-readings and re-receptions of their texts to discern how their teachings work together to shed light on the oneness of the Christian faith. Such re-readings and re-receptions do not suggest a failure of original readings and receptions; nor are they an *escamotage* [sleight of hand] used by theologians to paper over insurmountable theological problems.[8] Rather, returning to these

---

Toward an Ontology of Meaning," *Theological Studies* 71 (2010): 609–36. The sense that the council, while maintaining deep continuity with tradition, introduces elements that are discontinuous with what came before it is most often associated with Giuseppe Alberigo and Joseph A. Komanchak, eds., *History of Vatican II*, 5 vols. (Maryknoll, NY: Orbis Books, 1995–2006). Also critical to this perspective is David G. Schultenover, ed., *Vatican II: Did Anything Happen?* (New York: Continuum, 2007). The sense that there is no real rupture in Vatican II's documents is associated with Agostino Marchetto, *Il Concilio ecumenico Vaticano II: Contrappunto per la sua storia* (Vatican City: Liberia Editrice Vaticana, 2005). This work has been published in English as *The Second Vatican Ecumenical Council: A Counterpoint for the History of the Council* (Scranton, PA: University of Scranton Press, 2010).

[7] Despite the overall lack of attention to the relationship of Vatican I and Vatican II, there are some scholars who have noted its interpretive potential. Two critical sources on this topic are Hermann Pottmeyer, *Towards a Papacy in Communion: Perspectives from Vatican Councils I and II* (New York: Herder and Herder, 1998), and William Henn, *The Honor of My Brothers: A Brief History of the Relationship between the Pope and the Bishops* (New York: Crossroad, 2000). Some important texts on this issue are, Pottmeyer, "A New Phase in the Reception of Vatican II"; Pottmeyer, "The Petrine Ministry: Vatican I in the Light of Vatican II," in *Centro Pro Unione Bulletin* 65 (2004): 20–24; and Kasper, "Introduction to the Theme and Catholic Hermeneutics of the Dogmas of the First Vatican Council," in *The Petrine Ministry*, 7–23.

[8] Kasper, "Introduction to the Theme and Catholic Hermeneutics of the Dogma of the First Vatican Council," 13.

texts and engaging them anew is indicative of the way that Christian teachings are not merely stacked one upon the other but integrated into the life of the faithful through the spirit of Christ. Such re-readings and re-receptions are tasks that are characteristic of a community that witnesses to a living tradition. Kasper writes that:

> The concept of reception, which has often been neglected in the past, is fundamental for Catholic theology, particularly for ecumenical theology and the hermeneutics of dogmas. Such reception and re-reception do not mean questioning the validity of the affirmation of a Council; rather, they mean its acceptance on the part of the ecclesial community. This is not merely a passive and mechanical acceptance; rather, it is a living and creative process of appropriation and is therefore concerned with interpretation.[9]

Ongoing efforts to read and receive the teachings of ecumenical councils do not undermine the importance of earlier readings and receptions. The church must avoid the temptation of seeking to resolve the tensions between them too easily and instead strive to see their differences within the context of the profound realities that unite them.

I. Identity Crisis

The perceived incompatibility of Vatican I and Vatican II frustrates the church's ability to adequately interpret its own teachings and contradicts its own hermeneutic principles; it also hinders its capacity to speak meaningfully in the modern context. Attempts to polarize the teachings of Vatican I and Vatican II contribute to an identity crisis in the church described by Kasper.[10] Kasper argues that a fundamental aspect of the church's struggle to convey

---

[9] Ibid., 13.

[10] Kasper has a particularly interesting development of this argument in his article "Nature, Grace and Culture: On the Meaning of Secularization," in *Catholicism and Secularization in America*, ed. David Schindler (Notre Dame, IN: Communio Books, 1994), 31–51.

its message effectively today is that it does not know its own faith well enough to express it convincingly. While the church's difficulties are often attributed to outdated and otherwise ineffective presentations, Kasper argues that the problem also stems from internal tensions and a lack of clarity regarding critical elements of the church's own identity. This lack of self-understanding contributes to an impression that the church's message is at best incoherent and at worst contradictory. Ultimately, Kasper argues that the church must work to determine *what* it has to say to the modern world rather than just considering *how* to present its message.[11] It is important to clarify that Kasper's argument that the church must turn inward to achieve greater self-understanding so that it can speak meaningfully in the world does not exclude the opposite approach, namely, the need for the church to reach out to the world so that it might come to know its own identity more deeply. In other words, Kasper's call for the church to look *ad intra* to promote greater clarity *ad extra* is not exclusive of a recognition that the ecclesial community can often come to know itself most deeply, particularly through its encounters with those outside its visible boundaries. These two approaches are complementary, not mutually exclusive.

The inability to articulate a coherent relationship between Vatican I and Vatican II contributes to the church's "identity crisis" in at least four distinct ways. First, the fact that the church cannot see harmony between the positions of its two most recent ecumenical councils conveys the sense that it is unable to comprehend its own teachings and suffers from a critical lack of self-understanding. The perceived dichotomy between Vatican I and Vatican II forces believers into a type of schizophrenia or amnesia regarding the church's own most authoritative teachings. This unresolved tension also raises questions about whether the church is, in fact, guided by the Holy Spirit and a reliable teacher. If Vatican I and Vatican II cannot be reconciled, and Vatican I is deficient as some perceive, then can we say that the Spirit is always reliably present, especially in the work of councils? This calls into question the nature of the church's tradition and a core element of its identity.

---

[11] Kasper, "Nature, Grace and Culture: On the Meaning of Secularization," 32.

Second, the perception that Vatican I and Vatican II assert seemingly contradictory views on two of the most fundamental issues of the post-Enlightenment world, namely, authority and freedom, creates major problems for the church in the modern context. In order to speak meaningfully today, the church must offer a satisfying account of human freedom and demonstrate that authentic freedom is not inhibited by either divine providence or the exercise of ecclesial authority. Some fear that Vatican I's definition of papal infallibility is fundamentally irreconcilable with modern views of freedom so that its affirmation only confirms the incompatibility of the church's worldview with modern sensibilities. Ultimately, the church's apparent inability to offer a coherent account of authority and freedom, two loci which stand at the center of modern men's and women's self-understanding, fosters the sense that the church is a relic of a previous age and is incapable of providing satisfying answers to the most urgent contemporary questions.

A third way that the polarization of Vatican I and Vatican II contributes to the church's identity crisis is that it produces division within the Catholic community by creating a sense that members must choose *either* Vatican I's strong presentation of papal power *or* Vatican II's affirmation of collegiality. The impression that there are two distinct options or models of church leads to a sense that there is more than one type of Catholic—for example, a "Vatican II Catholic" or a "traditional Catholic"—and that one of these is more "authentically Catholic" than the other. This division weakens the church at a time when unity is desperately needed.

Finally, the perceived incompatibility of Vatican I and Vatican II generates critical problems in the ecumenical sphere. Issues of authority are at the heart of some of the most difficult ecumenical exchanges, and Vatican I's view of the papacy is often seen as "the largest and most scandalous stumbling block" to dialogue.[12] Marginalizing Vatican I's teachings as "not our real position" does not advance authentic dialogue but can only support facile agreements which distort Catholic positions and disrespects our dialogue partners. On the other side, insisting on Vatican I's model of the church as the only valid model, without reference to and

---

[12] Maximos Vgenopoulous, *Primacy in the Church from Vatican I to Vatican II* (Dekalb, IL: Northern Illinois University Press, 2013), 3.

integration with the larger conciliar tradition, presents a seemingly insurmountable obstacle in the quest for Christian unity. Pope John Paul II, in his encyclical *Ut Unum Sint*, rejected a rigid insistence on this model and advocated, instead, for the need to "find a way of exercising the primacy which, while in no way renouncing what is essential to its mission, is nonetheless open to a new situation (UUS 95)."[13] For ecumenical dialogue to flourish, the church must find ways to see Vatican I as part of a larger whole and demonstrate that it is compatible with the view of episcopal collegiality presented at Vatican II.

These four challenges, individually and collectively, create the impression that the church does not fully understand its own message and, as such, cannot serve as a fruitful dialogue partner or a valuable resource for modern men and women. Demonstrating core agreement between Vatican I's and Vatican II's presentations which appear, at best, in tension with one another and, at worst, in direct conflict would manifest an important step toward ameliorating the identity crisis in the church today and augment its ability to speak meaningfully to contemporary questions.

II. Hermeneutic Challenges

The failure to recognize a dynamic relationship between Vatican I and Vatican II stems largely from the fact that both have regularly been subjected to noncontextual readings. Interpreters of Vatican I and Vatican II have often approached the councils' teachings apart from their relation to particular historical and theological settings or have removed them from the wider context of a larger document or collection of documents. Additionally, as noted above, their teachings have often been considered apart from the conciliar tradition as a whole. As a result, neither council's teachings have been fully received as a body of texts that are

---

[13] John Paul II, Encyclical Letter *Ut Unum Sint* (On Commitment to Ecumenism), May 25, 1995, http://w2.vatican.va/content/john-paul-ii/en/encyclicals/documents/hf_jp-ii_enc_25051995_ut-unum-sint.html.

inherently connected, reflective of a particular historical and theological situation, and part of a larger theological tradition.

While both Vatican I and Vatican II suffer from inadequate, noncontextual readings, it is also the case that each has its own specific interpretive challenges. In regard to the interpretive problems associated with Vatican I, the extent of the misunderstandings of the council's teachings was captured by the late John Tracy Ellis, professor at The Catholic University of America, when he said, "It is doubtful that any event in the history of the modern Church ever gave rise to a greater flow of misinformation than the First Vatican Council."[14] According to Ellis "a web of error, misunderstanding and misinterpretation" surrounds Vatican I and has made it difficult to discern the council's true meaning and import for contemporary theological discussions.[15] A central difficulty fueling this misunderstanding is the fact that insufficient attention has been directed to the nature and intent of the council as a whole. Many studies of the First Vatican Council are, in fact, studies of the question of papal infallibility and are found in books about the issue of Petrine authority. The tremendous attention paid to the definition of papal infallibility in the fourth chapter of *Pastor Aeternus* has led to a lack of substantive engagement with the overall theology represented in the council's teachings.[16] Additionally, the fact that papal infallibility has often been assessed

---

[14] John Tracy Ellis, "The Church Faces the Modern World: The First Vatican Council," in *The General Council: Special Studies in Doctrinal and Historical Background*, ed. William McDonald (Washington, DC: The Catholic University of America Press, 1962), 135. Archbishop Kenrick of St. Louis also commented on the high degree of misinformation associated with Vatican I. His conclusion was that much of it was intentional. On returning from the council, he described it as "the one event in recent times, the history of which is most disputed and most studiously concealed from the knowledge of the public." See Peter Kenrick, *An Inside View of the Vatican Council* (New York: American Tract Society, 1871), 5.

[15] Ellis, "The Church Faces the Modern World," 135.

[16] Some notable exceptions to the dearth of substantive scholarship on the First Vatican Council as a whole include: Roger Aubert, *Vaticanum I* (Mainz: Matthias-Grünewald-Verlag, 1965); Cuthbert Butler, *The Vatican Council*, vols. 1 and 2 (London: Longmans, Green and Co., 1930); Klaus Schatz, *Vaticanum I 1869–70* (Paderborn: F. Schöningh, 1992); and Ulrich Horst, *Unfehlbarkeit und Geschichte* (Mainz: Matthias-Grüenewald-Verlag, 1982).

juridically rather than theologically has further contributed to the lack of a holistic reading of this council.

A second factor complicating the reception of Vatican I is the persistent sense that a maximalist interpretation of its texts represents the only proper reading of them. This perception gained prominence shortly after Pope Pius IX adjourned the council on October 20, 1870. A small number of church officials and scholars who avowed an extreme and rigid interpretation of Vatican I's definition of papal infallibility were quick to promote the view that the council had both ended conversations regarding the pope's power and effectively concluded all debate on authority in the church. They presented its texts not as one legitimate view of ecclesiastical power but as *the* definitive view. In other words, they sought to present Vatican I's teachings as "the definitive culmination of ecclesiology and the ecclesiastical order."[17] This position was held by only a small fraction of bishops at the council, but for a variety of reasons that will be explored later, it grew unchecked after the council's suspension. The way that the maximalist perspective has come to dominate the interpretation of Vatican I has given rise to the impression that the council presents papal power in a severe and unyielding way, one which is all but impossible to integrate with other models of ecclesial authority.[18]

Turning to Vatican II, a distinct interpretive challenge facing that council has been the long-dominant practice of generating separate commentaries on each of its documents as a means of disseminating their teachings. Even before the council's conclusion,

---

[17] Pottmeyer, *Towards a Papacy in Communion*, 111.

[18] Some, most notably Hans Küng, have raised questions over the legitimacy of Vatican I, given concerns about the level of freedom at the council. Thus, Küng would suggest that it is not that Vatican I has been underexamined but that it should be intentionally left out of the conversation all together. While the issues raised by Küng are important, it is not the case that they necessarily require a rejection of the council. Yves Congar made a similar assessment, noting that Küng's questions "invite us to a new 'reception' of the dogma of *Pastor Aeternus*, a 'reception' under new conditions thanks to a more comprehensive and better balanced ecclesiology, with a deeper knowledge of history, particularly that of the Roman See with the East." See Congar, "*Le journal de Mgr Darboy au concile du Vatican (1869–70)*," ed. André Duval and Yves Congar, *Revue des sciences philosopiques et théologiques* 54 (1970): 417.

there were many initiatives on the diocesan, national, and universal levels to publish texts to describe and interpret Vatican II's positions on topics such as the liturgy, the laity, revelation, and religious freedom. This method certainly bore fruit and played a critical role in the initial stages of the council's interpretation. The encapsulation of particular themes and individual texts, however, through lengthy commentaries, had the unintended double effects of distancing readers from the actual documents and obscuring the council's overall theology. This type of introduction to the council's work yielded the unfortunate result that "people acquired a somewhat overly abstract idea of Vatican II, as though it were simply a collection of texts, too abundant a collection!"[19] The council, for many, came to be understood as "nothing but words."[20] What was lacking was a theological perspective capable of integrating the council's diverse expressions by providing an overarching framework for its documents.[21]

Another impediment to Vatican II's interpretation arises from the documents themselves. While there is serious tension over how to best read and interpret the council's texts, it is also the case that there are significant tensions within the texts themselves. In other words, the tensions related to Vatican II's teachings are not only perceived—they are real. At various points between the conciliar documents, and even within particular documents themselves, seemingly conflicting positions are articulated and then left unresolved. This tension does not arise from an error but is a product of the fact that the council was content with "descriptive

[19] Alberigo, preface, *History of Vatican II*, 1:xi.

[20] Giuseppe Alberigo, *A Brief History of Vatican II* (Maryknoll, NY: Orbis Books, 2006), xiii.

[21] Many excellent studies on the interpretation of Vatican II have appeared in recent years including, Ormund Rush: *Still Interpreting Vatican II: Some Hermeneutical Principles* (New York: Paulist Press, 2004); Edward Hahnenberg, *A Concise Guide to the Documents of Vatican II* (Cincinnati, OH: St. Anthony Messenger Press, 2007); *Keys to the Council: Unlocking the Teaching of Vatican II*, ed. Catherine Clifford and Richard Gaillardetz (Collegeville, MN: Liturgical Press, 2012); Catherine Clifford, *Decoding Vatican II: Ecclesial Identity, Dialogue and Reform* (Paulist Press, 2014); and *Vatican II: Did Anything Happen?*, ed. David Schultenover (London: Bloomsbury Academic, 2007); Massimo Faggioli, *Vatican II: The Battle for Meaning* (New York: Paulist Press, 2012).

exposition rather than synthetic explanation."[22] It tolerated such tension because its goal was to hold up elements of the church's life, but "left it to theologians to construct a synthesis of them."[23] Given that real differences exist within Vatican II's texts, it is possible, and in many senses easier, to read the council's teachings selectively rather than holistically. By engaging in noncontextual readings of Vatican II, it is possible for multiple readers to find warrant for conflicting and even contradictory positions within its texts. As such, interpreters can argue for different positions from common readings of texts with each using compelling textual evidence as support. Without recourse to contextualized hermeneutics to determine which view constitutes the most appropriate reading of a particular passage, interpretations of conciliar texts can seem helplessly mired in irreconcilable differences of scholarly opinion.

Surveying the weaknesses and questions surrounding the interpretation of Vatican I and Vatican II, it becomes clear that their teachings are neither fully understood nor, consequently, fully received. Further contextualization is needed so that both councils can be interpreted more accurately. A deeper appreciation of each council, in turn, allows for the relationship between them to be seen more clearly and illumines critical aspects of the nature of the tradition of which they are both a part.

III. Looking at the Councils through the Lenses of *What, Why,* and *How*

This project seeks to transcend some of the interpretive problems that have plagued the reception of Vatican I and Vatican II—and blurred the nature of their relationship—by providing additional contextualization which allows for a more adequate interpretation of each council. This contextualization is achieved, largely, by expanding on two critical insights that have been developed in ef-

---

[22] Joseph Komonchak, "The Significance of Vatican Council II for Ecclesiology," in *The Gift of the Church: A Textbook on Ecclesiology*, ed. Peter Phan (Collegeville, MN: Liturgical Press, 2000), 69–92, at 76.

[23] Ibid., 76.

forts to advance the interpretation of Vatican II. The first, developed by John W. O'Malley, SJ, is that to understand *what* Vatican II teaches one must recognize *how* it expresses its teaching. In other words, one must attend to the form or style of conciliar documents and not merely their content in order to discern their meaning.[24] O'Malley argues that the authentic meaning of Vatican II's texts is often missed because their uniqueness is overlooked. For decades, scholars have attempted to employ hermeneutic strategies developed in relation to other councils in their efforts to interpret Vatican II's texts without realizing that the distinctive aspects of the council's content and style could not be fully appreciated through these conventional interpretive strategies. An adequate interpretation of Vatican II, according to O'Malley, demands that one look not only at *what* the council taught, namely, its content, but also at *how* it taught it—its style.

The second insight, offered by Steven Schloesser, SJ, extends O'Malley's provocative insight by emphasizing the role that Vatican II's historical location plays in determining what happened there.[25] Scholesser argues that Vatican II's break with the past is "painfully obvious" and, further, that O'Malley's work provides a "genuine revelation" for grasping this historical shift and its implications for the council's interpretation.[26] He notes that O'Malley's insight consists in recognizing *how* Vatican II broke with the past in some ways while still remaining faithful to the tradition. This change is epitomized by the council's move beyond the restrictive task of defining theological realities—which was what councils were "expected to do"—to employing the humanistic genre of epideictic oration.[27] After affirming

[24] John W. O'Malley has considered this question in several forums. Among these are, "Vatican II: Did Anything Happen?," *Theological Studies* 67 (March 2006): 3–33; and *What Happened at Vatican II* (Cambridge, MA: Harvard University Press, 2008).

[25] Stephen Schloesser, "Against Forgetting: Memory, History, Vatican II," *Theological Studies* 67 (2006): 275–319.

[26] Ibid., 276.

[27] O'Malley characterizes this expression as "a rhetoric of praise and congratulation" meant to "heighten appreciation for a person, an event, an institution, and to excite to the emulation of an ideal." See O'Malley, "Vatican II: Did Anything Happen?," 76.

O'Malley's advances, Schloesser builds on them by asking *why* Vatican II's changes were necessary. He writes:

> It is important to investigate *how* the council employed this genre. But it also seems important to survey *why* the council—in the years 1962 to 1965, framed by 1956 and 1968—needed to use such language. O'Malley has shifted our focus from *what* to *how*, from *content* to *form*. I would like to draw our attention from *form* to *content*—from *how* to *why*.[28]

Schloesser argues that O'Malley's perspectival step back from the council's content to consider its style invites another step back, this time to consider its historical context. He argues that the experiences and anxieties of a generation who lived during a time of "historical rupture" made the changes which took place not only possible but also an "ethical necessity."[29] This context constitutes a key factor in *why* the council taught what it taught. Schloesser thus adds to the contextualization begun by O'Malley by pointing out the importance of attending not only *what* the council taught and *how* it taught what it taught but also *why* it taught what it taught.

The present study expands O'Malley's and Scholesser's insights by directing questions of *what*, *why*, and *how* at Vatican I's texts and posing these questions to Vatican II in new and sharpened ways. To a greater extent than its successor, Vatican I has been subjected to ahistorical and atheological readings which have seriously distorted its interpretation. Engaging questions regarding Vatican I's context and style affords a fresh consideration of this complex council and its relation to its successor. This contextualization allows Vatican I's authentic voice to be heard and to speak more effectively in contemporary conversations. This rehabilitation of Vatican I initiates something of a chain reaction; specifically, the proper contextualization of Vatican I sheds considerable light on issues of *what* Vatican II taught, *how* Vatican II taught, and most important, *why* Vatican II taught. Seeing Vatican II against this new horizon in turn facilitates a greater awareness of the signifi-

---

[28] Schloesser, "Memory, History, Vatican II," 279; emphasis in the original.
[29] Ibid.

cance and the character of the conversations that have followed it. Thus, the end result of this chain reaction is not only an enhanced understanding of each of these councils and the developments which succeeded them but also a deepened understanding of the church itself. This increased self-understanding helps lead the church out of its identity crisis and, in turn, enhances its ability to convey its message more effectively.

After applying the questions of *what*, *why*, and *how* to Vatican I and Vatican II, one can see that various interpreters have often answered these questions incompletely, if not mistakenly. A proper contextualization of Vatican I and Vatican II in light of these questions illumines that the councils share many common questions, commitments, and proximities. Yet, it is also clear that these proximities and continuities exist amid significant differences. The challenge which arises is demonstrating the way in which the unity between Vatican I and Vatican II forms a shared horizon that is sufficiently strong to maintain their differences as complementary rather than mutually exclusive. Arriving at this goal requires contextualizing Vatican I and Vatican II in terms of *what*, *why*, and *how* so that our efforts to understand their relationship are guided by their authentic voices.

IV. Both Vatican I and Vatican II

Vatican I and Vatican II are connected by more than just St. Peter's Basilica. There would be grave consequences for our understanding of the church's nature and Christ's presence within it if geography were the only link between them. Hermann Pottmeyer captures the fundamental import of recognizing Vatican I and Vatican II as part of a single living tradition; he states, "Is Vatican II to be read in light of Vatican I, or is the direct opposite the case, or will the as yet unachieved reconciliation of the two councils show the necessity of a further stage in ecclesial self-understanding?"[30] What Pottmeyer's question probes, in part,

---

[30] Pottmeyer, "A New Phase in the Reception of Vatican II," 33.

is the question of whether the hermeneutic lenses and notion of catholicity that we apply to these councils are sufficiently flexible and inclusive in the catholic sense. In particular, is our approach to Vatican II adequately dynamic so that we can hold its teachings in tension with those of its predecessor, or do our lenses necessarily exclude them? Put another way, is the problem that a given text from Vatican I or Vatican II is inappropriate, or is it that the lenses by which we have approached them are inadequate? Showing the compatibility of Vatican I and Vatican II highlights the fact that expressing the fullness of the church's catholicity requires developing lenses for interpreting its tradition that are capable of integrating all its legitimate elements. Developing such lenses, as Pottmeyer suggests, has the power to inaugurate a "new phase of ecclesial self-understanding."[31]

This book is about Vatican I and Vatican II and their relationship, but it is also about the nature of the church as a whole. It argues that achieving greater self-understanding regarding these issues enhances the church's ability to speak meaningfully today by providing satisfying answers to urgent questions posed by modern men and women. Doing so does not imply that no differences exist between Vatican I and Vatican II or that their points of contrast can be resolved with a theological *escamotage*. Highlighting the relationship between these councils does not mean that Vatican I is free from interpretive or substantive challenges or that its teachings are as adequate as Vatican II's. On the contrary, this book seeks to understand what can be learned from these councils, and the conciliar tradition in general, by seeking to integrate their apparently divergent positions within a greater theological reality. This study develops a more adequate understanding of the relationship between Vatican I and Vatican II which is consistent with the church's own long-standing principles of dogmatic interpretation and consonant with a vibrant sense of catholicity as a *both/and* rather than an *either/or* reality. It is only in recognizing *both* Vatican I *and* Vatican II as contributing essential insights into the nature of the church that its true nature and the mystery at its heart can be preserved.

---

[31] Ibid.

This book explores the relationship between Vatican I and Vatican II and the way in which this relationship is representative of the church's living tradition. Nevertheless, the study does not examine and interpret every text belonging to these councils. For example, Vatican I has two constitutions—*Dei Filius* (Dogmatic Constitution on Catholic Faith) and *Pastor Aeternus* (Dogmatic Constitution on the Church). Here, we will only consider the latter. Additionally, the study will focus on Vatican II's *Lumen Gentium* (Dogmatic Constitution on the Church) and even more specifically, its treatment of ecclesial authority. In many ways, the argument about the relationship between Vatican I and Vatican II could be expanded to *Dei Filius* and *Dei Verbum* (Dogmatic Constitution on Divine Revelation). This study has elected to examine specific questions which motivated the council's larger purpose as well as those that affect unitive themes in their texts. To that end, *Pastor Aeternus* and *Lumen Gentium* receive primary attention because they offer the greatest potential for direct and fruitful comparisons. While a focused concentration on select texts runs the risk of non-contextual readings—the very thing this study seeks to overcome—it also has the potential to establish a vital lens for reading, relating, and interpreting the larger corpus of texts from both councils. This book thus aims to elucidate a way of understanding and relating Vatican I and Vatican II through a comparative reading of *Pastor Aeternus* and *Lumen Gentium* which may then be applied more broadly to the rich teachings found in both councils. In this case, setting aside cross-comparisons among all eighteen major texts (two from Vatican I and sixteen from Vatican II) clears the way for focus on key points of connection, making it possible to introduce a new hermeneutic for reading the councils as part of a common tradition.

Chapters 2 and 3 seek to achieve a greater contextualization of the First Vatican Council. Chapter 2 directs Scholesser's question of *why* at Vatican I, examining the way that serious external and internal threats motivated the calling of the council and the character of its response. Chapter 3 applies the questions of *how* and *what* to *Pastor Aeternus* to consider the ways that readings of the council have often misunderstood its content and the genre of its teachings. The fourth chapter examines the period immediately following Vatican I and the way in which the council's immediate reception informs later understandings of its texts and their proper interpretation. Attention then turns in the fifth and sixth chapters to Vatican II. Chapter 5 looks at the issue of *why* Vatican II taught what it taught in light of an enhanced understanding of Vatican I and its legacy. Chapter 6 builds on chapter 5 and examines the ways in which *what* and *how* Vatican II taught are compatible with the teachings of its predecessor. It highlights the continuity between Vatican I's and Vatican II's presentations of ecclesial authority by comparing elements of style and content in *Pastor Aeternus* and *Lumen Gentium* 18–23. The seventh and final chapter leverages the insights of the preceding ones to discern the nature of the relationship between Vatican I and Vatican II as well as the character of the church's living tradition. Attention to this tradition suggests that recent developments in the reception of Vatican II, as well as many present-day questions about ecclesiology, authority, and freedom, constitute natural extensions of conversations undertaken at Vatican I and continued at Vatican II.

CHAPTER TWO

The Historical and Theological Setting of Vatican I

The question before the council fathers was: Should the church, at a time when the world was in turmoil, locate itself primarily beneath the standard of a fixed and unchangeable authority or present itself more as a historical reality also subject to history and even to change—should it accept the modern development of liberty as something in accord with the gospel?[1]

—Klaus Schatz

Much of the work of understanding Vatican I and its relationship with Vatican II centers around retrieving the former from the margins of theological discourse through engaging in re-readings and re-receptions of its decrees. This rehabilitation requires disentangling the web of misinformation surrounding the council by contextualizing it both historically and theologically. Doing so allows for Vatican I's voice to enter contemporary conversations more productively. This chapter provides such contextualization

---

[1] Klaus Schatz, *Papal Primacy: From Its Origins to the Present*, trans. John Otto and Linda M. Maloney (Collegeville, MN: Liturgical Press, 1996), 156. Joseph Burgess summed up this sentiment even more succinctly when he wrote that "above all, the council concerned the question of questions, whether liberalism and Catholicism should be reconciled." See Joseph Burgess, "The Historical Background of Vatican I," in *Teaching Authority and Infallibility in the Church*, ed. Paul Empie, T. Austin Murphy, and Joseph Burgess (Minneapolis, MN: Augsburg, 1980), 294.

by directing at Vatican I aspects of the *"why"* question raised by Schloesser at the texts of Vatican I. *Why was Vatican I called? Why did defining papal infallibility seem to pose the best response to the challenges of the day?* This examination will show that it is a misunderstanding of *why* Vatican I taught what it taught that serves as a key source of the council's misinterpretation.

Distanced from the setting in which its texts were formulated, many people assume that Vatican I was initially and principally concerned with defining papal infallibility, indeed with defining it in the most rigid and extreme way possible. This presumption exerts a distorting effect on the council's texts that has long hindered their interpretation. By examining Vatican I in its proper setting, it becomes clear that defining papal infallibility was, in fact, not the council's original goal and not the product of a unanimously shared ecclesiology among the council fathers. A contextualized reading reveals that while Vatican I's definition of papal infallibility responds to a pressing question, the question most of the council fathers sought to answer was not a theological one about the nature of the pope's authority but a strategic one concerning ecclesial authority in the face of serious internal and external threats. As Schatz indicates, the real issue before the council fathers at Vatican I regarded how the church should locate itself in relation to the seismic shifts reshaping modern society. Should the church show itself as amenable to these changes or reject them? Establishing Vatican I's context and intent—*why* it taught what it taught—sheds considerable light on the council's teachings and demonstrates that they are open to a significantly broader interpretation than they have generally received.

I. Setting the Context of the Council:
The Three Traumas of Rome

As with any council, Vatican I's history is complicated and includes a diverse range of political, historical, and theological influences. In the decades leading up to this gathering, a myriad of factors—or "traumas" as they are described by Hermann Pottmeyer—contributed to an increasingly defensive sensibility in Rome.[2] These traumas were ecclesial, political, and philosophical in nature. Fear catalyzed by these developments fueled the quest for a council and shaped its deliberations in profound ways.

The first trauma facing the church was ecclesial in character and grew out of debates in the fourteenth and fifteenth centuries which came to a head particularly in the Great Schism (1378–1417) and lingered thereafter in a series of contests over papal and conciliar authority. At the center of the controversy lay the question of who holds supreme authority in the church—the pope, a council united with the pope, or a council, if necessary, acting without the pope? This dispute saw increasingly well-developed models of conciliarism emerge as one approach to resolving the escalating confrontations.[3] While multiple expressions of conciliarism emerged, each reflecting somewhat different understandings of the relationship between the pope and the bishops, as a whole this theory sought to retrieve elements of the *communio* notion of the first millennium, which emphasized the responsibility of the episcopal college for the universal church and the power of individual bishops to govern their dioceses.[4] As their name suggests, a primary commitment of this group was retrieving the ancient practice of convening councils to adjudicate significant questions regarding the church's identity. The conciliarist view was perceived as a threat by Rome not only because it posed a challenge to papal power but also because Rome saw it as a hindrance to the church's ability to act quickly and decisively when its own interests were endangered.

---

[2] See Pottmeyer, "The Three Traumas of Rome," in *Towards a Papacy in Communion*, 36–50.

[3] On the rise of conciliarism, see Brian Tierny, *Foundations of the Conciliar Theory: The Contribution of the Medieval Canonists from Gratian to the Great Schism* (Cambridge, UK: Cambridge University Press, 2010), and Peter Oakley, *The Conciliarist Tradition: Constitutionalism in the Catholic Church 1300–1870* (Oxford: Oxford University Press, 2008).

[4] For an examination of particular forms of conciliarism, see *The Church, The Councils and Reform*, ed. Gerald Christianson, Thomas Izbicki, and Christopher Belitto (Washington, DC: The Catholic University of America Press, 2008), and *Conciliarism and Papalism*, ed. J. H. Burns and Thomas Izbicki (Cambridge, UK: Cambridge University Press, 1998).

Questions regarding the balance of authority between the pope and the bishops were manifest in particularly challenging ways by French Gallicanism.[5] The Gallicanists were adamant that supreme authority rests in the consensus of the whole church and that the pope, while having legitimate primacy of jurisdiction, is not superior by himself to the church as a whole. The Gallican movement represented a growing sentiment that late medieval and early modern iterations of papal authority were inconsistent with the patrimony of the ancient church. Moreover, many Gallican conciliarists argued that, while it was important to maintain the "essential rights" of the papacy, the proliferation and formalization of "accidental rights" should be rejected.[6] In an effort to capture what lay at the heart of Gallicanism, Congar summarized the position of this group as "the will not to let the pole *Ecclesia* be absorbed by the pole *papacy*."[7] Gallicanism presented a serious challenge for Rome in that it not only advanced a theological position but also carried significant political dimensions with it as well. In certain key ways, Gallican interests aligned with those of secular leaders who sought to curtail Rome's influence within their territories. Gallican efforts to limit the pope's powers seemed to support claims by certain states, such as France, to have control over the national churches within their jurisdictions. Several key tenets of the Gallican position were formalized in the Four Gallican Articles passed by the Assembly of French Clergy in 1682.[8] Among other things, these articles asserted that the pope had power only in regard to spiritual affairs and that his teachings were not irreformable until they had received the consent of the church. The confrontational nature of these assertions and their tacit support of its political adversaries set Rome in an increasingly

[5] For an excellent study of Gallicanism, see Richard F. Costigan, *The Consensus of the Church and Papal Infallibility: A Study in the Background of Vatican I* (Washington, DC: The Catholic University of America Press, 2005).

[6] See Costigan, *The Consensus of the Church and Papal Infallibility*, 140.

[7] Yves Congar, "*Gallicanisme*," in *Catholicisme*, ed. G. Jacquemet (Paris: Letouzey, 1956), 4:1736.

[8] See Aimé-Georges Martimort, *Le Gallicanisme* (Paris: Presses universitaires de France, 1973).

defensive posture against movements which seemed to restrict papal primacy.

A second and parallel trauma confronting Rome presented itself from the political realm as the system of a state-controlled church. This structure was characterized by an extensive dependence by bishops on monarchs and elements of the state bureaucracy, a situation which had long been growing in Europe but reached a climax at the time of the French Revolution.[9] The Revolution devastated the dominant social, political, and ecclesiastical orders of France and pulled much of Europe into this process of change. It eliminated the obstacles presented by the *Ancien Régime* and advanced the call for republican democracies to replace it throughout the continent. An emerging philosophical and practical separation between the church and the state displaced long-standing models of integrated unity between them. For the church, an immediate effect of these shifts was that many of its remaining traditional civil prerogatives and properties were eliminated or replaced by secular authorities. While in recent centuries the church had wielded a temporal authority which equaled or surpassed that of the state, in the wake of the Revolution, its authority was seriously limited and the church was even, in several key ways, subjected to control by national governments. This limiting of the church's role and the advent of increased governmental interference not only restrained the church's authority and independence but also eliminated key sources of income on which it depended.[10]

Significant losses in the political sphere not only hindered the church's ability to conduct its affairs and diminished its influence but also produced major psychological obstacles. In the mind-set

---

[9] Schatz observes the way developments stemming from the French Revolution catalyzed the conditions that brought about the council's convocation; he writes, "There can scarcely have been any event in history that was so important in laying the groundwork for the ultimate victory of the papacy at Vatican I as the French Revolution of 1789." See Schatz, *Papal Primacy*, 143. An important source on connections between developments in the church and the French Revolution is Gotham Parsons, *The Church and the Republic: Gallicanism and Political Ideology in Renaissance France* (Washington, DC: The Catholic University of America Press, 2004).

[10] See Auber, *"Welt und Kirche am Vorabend des Konzils,"* in *Vaticanum* I, 9–46.

of this period, there was a close association between temporal and spiritual power. The church's strength and legitimacy as a teacher were tied, in part, to its ability to act without the constraint of external forces. There was an assumption, at least among Christian peoples and nations, that ecclesiastical authority had claim to a certain type of autonomy given the sense that, as the authoritative communicator of God's will on earth, it was not subject in many arenas to the decisions of other temporal powers. Thus, the subjection of the church to state bureaucracies, as had transpired in France, catalyzed deep feelings of alarm and insecurity within the Christian community, inasmuch as the loss of autonomy in its affairs seemed to diminish its ability to speak authoritatively on spiritual matters. Anxiety about the church's position in relation to the political or civil sphere fueled a growing quest for security or control, eloquently termed by Ulrich Horst as *Sicherheitsdenken* (security-mentality).[11] The church's sense of insecurity reached a climax in the Vatican's battle to resist the unification of Italy and the loss of its autonomous Papal States. The Papal States had been restored in 1849 but were subsequently reduced to Rome and its environs in 1860. The question of whether the church would be able to retain this territory permanently with the limited resources at its disposal was the cause of tremendous anxiety in Rome and influenced its thinking on a broad range of concerns.[12]

---

[11] For Horst's treatment of this sense of insecurity see his *Unfehlbarkeit und Geschichte: Studien zur Unfehlbarkeitsdiskussion von Melchior Cano bis zum I. Vatikanischen Konzil* (Mainz: Matthias-Grunewald-Verlag, 1982).

[12] The extent to which the threat to the Papal States influenced the conversation about papal infallibility has been debated. On the urgency of this matter Hans Küng has written, "In Rome, the Roman question overshadowed everything else; the question, that is to say, whether the Papal States, which had been restored in 1849 but had been reduced to Rome and its immediate neighborhood by the intervention of the Piedmontese government in 1860 and were notorious everywhere for their monsignorial mismanagement and social backwardness, would have to be given up or whether it would be possible to hold onto them permanently, with nothing but French support to rely on in the face of the Italian unification movement which wanted Rome for its capital. Almost the only ray of hope for those, who relying on Matthew 16:18, wanted at all costs to hold on to temporal power was the idea that no one would dare to take action against a pope whose infallibility had been solemnly proclaimed *urbi et orbi* in ecumenical

In this context of fear and instability—and amid the vacuum of power among the national churches—many turned to Rome as the one remaining power in Europe capable of restoring order.[13] The concentration of hopeful expectations in the Vatican became known as "Ultramontanism" in that it looked "beyond the Alps" for a solution to the contemporary crisis.[14] This centripetal movement was allowed to intensify without counterweight inasmuch as it encountered minimal resistance from the national churches. Many bishops who had long resisted efforts to consolidate the church's authority in Rome were now, largely, eager for papal intervention to help salvage their losing campaigns in many local territories. Moreover, Europe's aristocracy and nobility wanted a restoration of their political power by means of a reuniting of "the throne and altar." To this end, the Congress of Vienna was convened from September 1814 to June 1815.

While it has often been suggested that the rise of Roman centralization in the eighteenth and nineteenth centuries was instigated by the Vatican as a means of aggrandizing its own power, historical evidence suggests that this movement drew its momentum primarily from individuals and groups throughout Europe turning to Rome for assistance. This dynamic was astutely observed by Alexis de Tocqueville in 1856 when he observed that the move toward Vatican centralization was "a matter more of the pope being compelled by the faithful to become absolute master of the church than of the faithful being compelled by him to become his subordinates."[15] The threatening political situation led many to support endowing the pope with an absolute sovereignty similar to that enjoyed by some of his secular counterparts so that

---

council." See: Hans Küng, *Infallible?: An Unresolved Inquiry* (New York: Seabury Press, 1994), 74. Others, such as Schatz, have downplayed the influence of the question of the Papal States on Rome's approach to theological questions.

[13] A useful survey of this development can be found in Schatz's section, "From the French Revolution to Vatican I," in *The Origins of Papal Primacy*, 143–55.

[14] On the development of the Ultramontanist position see: *Varieties of Ultramontanism*, ed. J. van Arx (Washington, DC: The Catholic University of America Press, 1998).

[15] Quoted in Emile Ollivier, *L'église et l'état au Concile du Vatican* (Paris: *Garnier frères*, 1879), 314.

he might act without constraint to protect the church when necessary. An additional benefit of such a solution, from Rome's perspective, was that it also had the potential to ameliorate internal challenges by definitively deciding the question of who served as the court of last resort in the church. Granting absolute sovereignty to the pope served as a strong and clear rejection of the Gallicanists' claims that the pope's teachings required the assent of the universal church before they could be seen as irreformable. Ultimately, the erosion of the church's temporal power by secular authorities and the growing volatility of Europe catalyzed tremendous fear in Rome which significantly impacted its thinking and its actions throughout the nineteenth century.

A third and final source of trauma for Rome was the ascendance of rationalism and liberalism. In addition to the social and political changes ushered in by the French Revolution, this period also represents a climax in the elevation of unaided human reason as the source of all authority. Prior to the Enlightenment, the church had enjoyed a position of teaching authority which included the capacity to assimilate and interpret advances in all fields of human inquiry. The advent of rationalism called this privileged position into question by asserting human reason as the ultimate authority and challenging the reliability of divine revelation as known in the church's Scripture and tradition. Revealed religion, and all authorities rooted in revelation, was subjected to severe skepticism and often rejected in favor of rational analysis and the type of empirically verifiable knowledge provided by the sciences. As such, the church found itself set in unaccustomed conflict with scientific inquiry and often saw its voice shunted to the margins of intellectual discourse, particularly when questions of authority or epistemological reliability were at stake.[16] These developments were perceived by many in the church as posing a threat of an

---

[16] For two interesting studies on the church's movement to the margins of discourse, see: William Plachter, *The Domestication of Transcendence: How Modern Thinking about God Went Wrong* (Louisville, KY: Westminster John Knox Press, 1996), and Michael Buckley, *At the Origins of Modern Atheism* (New Haven, CT: Yale University Press, 1990). For a shorter examination of this topic, see Giuseppe Alberigo, "The Authority of the Church in the Documents of Vatican I and Vatican II," in *Journal of Ecumenical Studies* 19 (1982): 119–45.

entirely different order and magnitude than past challenges. Rather than calling into question any one particular doctrine as previous heresies had done, the proponents of liberal thought challenged the church's ability to teach at all.

Pope Gregory XVI's encyclical *Mirari Vos* (On Liberalism and Religious Indifferentism), published on August 15, 1832, spoke vividly of the magnitude of the dangers to the church posed by rationalism. Gregory writes:

> We speak of the things which you see with your own eyes, which We both bemoan. Depravity exults; science is impudent; liberty, dissolute. The holiness of the sacred is despised; the majesty of divine worship is not only disapproved by evil men, but defiled and held up to ridicule. Hence sound doctrine is perverted and errors of all kinds spread boldly. The laws of the sacred, the rights, institutions, and discipline—none are safe from the audacity of those speaking evil. Our Roman See is harassed violently and the bonds of unity are daily loosened and severed. The divine authority of the Church is opposed and her rights shorn off. She is subjected to human reason and with the greatest injustice exposed to the hatred of the people and reduced to vile servitude. The obedience due bishops is denied and their rights are trampled underfoot. Furthermore, academies and schools resound with new, monstrous opinions, which openly attack the Catholic faith; this horrible and nefarious war is openly and even publicly waged. Thus, by institutions and by the example of teachers, the minds of the youth are corrupted and a tremendous blow is dealt to religion and the perversion of morals is spread. So the restraints of religion are thrown off, by which alone kingdoms stand.[17]

[17] A similar description is offered by Cardinal Henry Edward Manning, who wrote in his book *The True Story of the Vatican Council* that "the bishops note that in our time there exists no new or special heresy in matters of faith, but rather a universal perversion and confusion of first truths and principles which assail the foundations of truth and the preambles of all belief. That is to say, as doubt attacked faith, unbelief has avenged faith by destroying doubt. Men cease to doubt what they disbelieve outright. They have come to deny that the light of nature and the evidences of creation prove the existence of God. They deny, therefore, the existence of God, the existence of the soul, the dictates of conscience, of right and wrong, and of the moral law. If there be no God, there is no legislator, and their morality is independent of any lawgiver, and exists in and by itself, or rather has no existence except subjectively in individuals, by customs inherited from conventional use and the mental habits of society. They note the wide-spread denial of any supernatural order, and therefore existence of faith.

Following Gregory, many ecclesial leaders reasoned that rationalism seemed poised to dismantle the church's authority and traditional structures so that it had to be resisted at all costs. Rome was so traumatized by the force and destructive potential of these ideas that it was not optimistic about the possibility of dialogue with them and resisted their penetration into the church's thinking. Therefore, instead of seeking some form of reconciliation, Rome devoted its energies to defining the church against the worldview that was emerging.

Vatican I's teachings cannot be properly understood apart from the context of fear and insecurity wrought by the traumas emanating from the ecclesial, political, and philosophical spheres. In response to these forces, Rome adopted a thoroughly defensive posture which dominated its self-understanding and view of the world in the years leading up to Vatican I. The issues which the church in the nineteenth century sought to engage were not solely theological but also political and philosophical in nature. Accordingly, the council's teachings should not be seen as purely theological in nature. Ultimately, *why* Vatican I taught what it taught was not merely to provide clarity on theological questions. Its teachings also served as means of preserving the church's authority and independence in an environment that it perceived as increasingly hostile to its existence.

II. Providing in an
"Extraordinary Way for an Extraordinary Need":
The Idea of Convening a Council

Pius IX first formally introduced the possibility of a council on December 6, 1864. During a meeting of the Congregation of Rites, the pope dismissed all the officials present in order to speak

---

They refer to the assertion that science is the only truth which is positive, and to the alleged sufficiency of human reason for the life and destinies of man, or, in other words, deism, independent morality, secularism, and rationalism which has invaded every country west of Europe." Edward Manning, *The True Story of the Vatican Council* (London: Burns, 1877), 25–26.

privately with the cardinals. Once alone, he conveyed to them that he was contemplating convening a meeting of the universal church in order to "provide in this extraordinary way for the extraordinary needs of the Christian flock."[18] Pius instructed those gathered to submit to him, in the greatest secrecy, their thoughts about the potential benefit and feasibility of such an undertaking. Later, he extended this request to a select group of bishops. Interestingly, Pius's announcement that he was considering a council took place only two days prior to the publication of "The Syllabus of Errors" on December 8, 1864. This document condemned eighty errors of nineteenth-century Liberalism such as rationalism, freedom of speech, atheism, divorce, and the separation of church and state. The last error sought to cement the polarization of the church and the world by condemning the suggestion that "the Roman Pontiff can and ought to reconcile himself and come to terms with progress, liberalism and modern civilization."[19] The proximity of Pius's announcement and the publication of the Syllabus signaled to many that the council would serve as a way of confirming and expanding on the errors that had been only outlined.

While the pope's announcement in December 1869 marks the first public disclosure of his thoughts about a council, there is evidence indicating that he had long been considering such a move. The first record of Pius's interest in gathering the bishops exists in a letter of Cardinal Luigi Lambruschini of Italy who recorded that he and Pius had spoken about such a possibility as early as May 1849.[20] Lambruschini wrote that he had recommended to Pius that "like the national councils called to remedy particular ills facing the churches, the pope should call a general council to answer the needs of the whole church."[21] Other bishops also testified to discussing this topic with Pius while in Rome to

[18] Butler, *The Vatican Council*, 1:81.

[19] "*Syllabus Pii IX*," in *Enchiridion Symbolorum, Definitiorum de Rebus Fidei et Morum*, ed. Henricus Denzinger and Adolfus Schonmetzer, 33rd ed. (Rome: Herder, 1965), 584.

[20] Luigi Lambruchini (1776–1854) was secretary of state for Gregory XVI. His letter is included in Frederick Cwiekowski, *The English Bishops and the First Vatican Council* (Louvain: Publications Universitaires de Louvain, 1971), 61.

[21] Cwiekowski, *The English Bishops and the First Vatican Council*, 63.

celebrate the canonization of the Japanese martyrs in 1862.[22] One of the most informative and interesting descriptions of such an exchange is that of Cardinal Nicholas Wiseman of England who reported to the *Tablet* that he had spoken with Pius about the potential benefit of a council a year prior to the pope's announcement. The *Tablet*'s account states:

> The Sovereign Pontiff has long entertained the desire to hold an Oecumnical Council as one of the most efficacious remedies that can be applied to the evils which afflict the Church throughout the world. H[is] E[minence] the late Cardinal Wiseman, when in Rome in 1863, urged upon the Pope his own view of the great blessings which might flow from a General Council. The Pontiff then replied that the subject was occupying his mind, and that he was recommending it to God; but that he feared his own great age offered an obstacle to his beginning so anxious and laborious an undertaking.[23]

While the exact sequence of Pius's reflections is difficult to establish, his extended deliberations on the prospect of a council suggest a long-standing concern for the gravity of the church's situation. That, for fifteen years, from the early part of his papacy, Pius wrestled with the idea of gathering the bishops, indicates that the church's precarious status weighed heavily on him and served as a focus of his pontificate.[24]

---

[22] These testimonies are recorded in: Joannes Dominicus Mansi, *Sacrorum conciliorum nova et amplissimi collection* (hereafter Mansi), 53 vols. (Graz: Akademische Druck u. Verlagsanstalt, 1961).

[23] The *Tablet* (February 20, 1869). It is interesting to note that a similar concern about advanced age weighed on John XXIII in his discernment about calling a council.

[24] On Pius IX's decision to call a council, see Battista Mondin, *The Popes of the Modern Ages: From Pius IX to John Paul II* (Vatican City: Urbaniana University Press, 2004). Here, Mondin writes: "The transition from a still essentially Constantinian concept of the Church to a Church exclusively founded on the Spirit could not be a sudden affair or a painless operation. To Pius IX fell the hard and thankless task of managing this painful transition" (16). Another important source on this topic is Roger Aubert, *Le pontificat de Pie IX*, vol. 21 of *Histoire de l'Eglise*, ed. Augustin Fliche and Victor Matron (Paris: Bloud et Gay, 1952), 262–310. An interesting English-language biography on Pius IX that focuses on this aspect of his papacy is Frank Coppa, *Pope Pius IX: Crusader in a Secular Age* (Boston: Twayne Publishers, 1979).

The majority of those who submitted responses to Pius's request strongly supported his initiative.[25] What is most striking in reading these letters is that they are nearly unanimous in communicating a sense that serious and unprecedented issues faced the church. Several conveyed the impression that the situation was so dire as to be potentially apocalyptic. Eugenio Cecconi, the archbishop of Florence who was charged by Pius to write a history of the council, notes that the responses indicate two main premises from which the destructive tendencies of the age flow. He identifies these premises as the following: "One that society, as such, has no duties towards God, religion being an affair of the individual conscience only; the other that human reason is sufficient to itself, and that a supernatural order, by which men are elevated to a higher knowledge and destiny either does not exist, or is at least beyond the cognisanse [sic] and care of civil society."[26] The majority of the respondents agreed with the pope's assessment that contemporary circumstances warranted the extraordinary act of convening an ecumenical council for only the twentieth time in the church's history. Such a gathering would allow for a strong and united response to the powerful forces confronting the Christian community.

While most of those consulted supported the idea of a conciliar remedy, a minority opposed such a solution. This minority also expressed deep concerns about the church's precarious position in modern society; the same diagnosis of the "disturbed state of the world" which led the majority to support a council, however, led the minority to question the prudence of gathering the universal church at the present moment. The minority argued that the climate was too chaotic for productive collaboration by the bishops and the situation too dangerous for them to absent themselves from their dioceses. They also worried that a council could further antagonize the heads of governments and encourage them to exert even harsher measures against the national churches.

---

[25] These responses can be found in Mansi, XLIX, 9–94. They are also presented in F. Van der Horst, *Das Schema über die Kirche auf dem 1 Vaticanischen Konzil* (Paderborn: Verlag Bonifacius-Druckerei, 1963), 20–25.

[26] Cecconi's summary is found in Manning, *True Story of the Vatican Council*, 5.

Another concern was that the type of doctrinal formulations that
would likely develop at a gathering convened in the current state
of fear would only alienate modern men and women by providing
evidence of exactly the type of outdated thinking of which the
church was accused. Fearing that a "doctrinal response" was the
wrong approach, James A. Corcoran, a theologian and priest from
the Diocese of Charleston, expressed his misgivings in a letter to
Matron J. Spaulding, archbishop of Baltimore; he stated, "If it were
left to these theologians the nineteenth [*sic*] ecumenical council
would issue more decrees, I mean more *doctrinal definitions*, than
all its predecessors from Nicaea to Trent."[27] Ultimately, the minority's opposition to a council was not an indication that it did not
recognize the severity of the situation; rather, its resistance was
rooted in a belief that there was a more effective way of dealing
with it.

While the majority and minority responses were nearly unanimous in affirming the gravity of the challenges facing the church,
they do not reflect a consensus on what represented the most
pressing manifestation of this danger. In other words, the letters
point to the egregious character of contemporary errors, but they
do not agree on their concrete expressions. When asked to indicate
the most serious concerns of the day, the respondents offer a wide
scope of opinions. Some of the chief problems identified were
"pantheism, naturalism, rationalism, socialism, communism,
spiritism, religious indifference; also the modern Protestant and
rationalistic teachings in regard to the inspiration of the Sacred
Books, their authority and interpretation."[28] The difficulty in identifying the specific problems to be addressed foreshadowed some
of the complexity that the council itself would face. Most councils
in the church's history had been gathered in response to a "clear
and present" danger, and thus the task of developing an agenda
was relatively straightforward. The task before Vatican I was more
amorphous in that the threats facing the church were not directed
at particular positions; rather, they constituted intellectual and

---

[27] See Ellis, "The Church Faces the Modern World," 125–26.

[28] This summary is Butler's and is found in his chapter, "Preparations at Rome,"
in *The Vatican Council*, 1:83.

political trends that informed a wide span of dogmatic, practical, and sociopolitical issues. What had been called into question was not a specific teaching but the legitimacy of the church's authority and, ultimately its very existence. Therefore, from its very early stages, there was a sense that certain elements of the upcoming council would be unique in the church's history.

It is significant to note that very few of the letters submitted to Pius about the possibility of calling a council raise the topic of papal infallibility, much less recommend it as a central theme for the gathering. Only a handful of the bishops and cardinals surveyed even mention this issue. In general, these letters convey a desire for Rome to shore up its teachings and assert its own authority, but they do not recommend how the council might achieve such aims. The cardinals and bishops who responded positively to the idea of a council did not tie their support to the idea of advancing a particular teaching; instead, they were motivated by the need to halt the proliferation of modern errors. Some expressed a belief that the best means of responding to contemporary challenges would become clear in the course of the council through the assistance of the Holy Spirit. One cardinal's reply indicates as much in noting that "God, who has suggested to your Holiness the thought of an Ecumenical Council to raise a strong defense against the vast evils of our time, will make the way plain, overcome all difficulties, and give to your Holiness and the bishops a moment of truce; peace, and time enough to fulfill so great a work."[29] The fact that the bishops do not identify the issue of papal infallibility as a topic for discussion suggests that in the council's initial development, the question of the pope's power was viewed as one theme on the horizon of the much larger issue of the church's authority and independence. In other words, *why* the bishops supported the idea of calling a council was as a means of preserving the church's freedom, independence, and ability to teach authoritatively. *How* this would be achieved was not yet determined.

[29] Manning, *True Story of the Vatican Council*, 10.

III. The Intent of the Council Manifest in *Aeterni Patris*

On June 29, 1868, Pius IX issued the pastoral letter, *Aeterni Patris*, convoking the Vatican Council. The letter presents the decision to gather the universal church as harmonious with the ancient Christian tradition of convening ecumenical councils "in periods of calamity" so that the bishops might "prudently and wisely agree upon all those measures that can help clarify dogmas of the faith; stamp out rampant errors; propagate, explain, and develop Catholic doctrine; protect and restore ecclesiastical discipline; and reform corrupt morals."[30] Corresponding to this tradition and to advice received from the cardinals and bishops, Pius notes that the upcoming council would seek to calm the "fearful tempest" threatening the Christian community by asserting clear dogmatic formulations in order to express Catholic teaching with "the greatest accuracy" (AP, 13).

The tone of *Aeterni Patris* is characterized by two polarized extremes. On the one hand, it reflects intense pessimism and hostility regarding the direction of modern developments. On the other hand, it expresses supreme confidence in the church's ability to overcome its opponents. These two poles set the tone for the antithetical vision of the church-world relationship which characterizes the document. In regard to the first extreme, much of *Aeterni Patris* is dedicated to describing the beleaguered state of the church and the affronts it had endured at the hands of the "violent enemies of God" (AP, 13). Faced with a "mass of calamities," the council would work to "repair the ruins of the Church, attend to the salvation of the Lord's flock, and repel the destructive attacks and efforts of those who would destroy completely civil society and, if it were possible, the church herself" (AP, 14). The sense of an apocalyptic assault on the Christian community is dramatically conveyed throughout the text. This impression is vividly communicated in its statement that:

---

[30] All quotes from *Aeterni Patris* are taken from *Documents of Vatican Council I, 1869–70*, ed. John F. Broderick (Collegeville, MN: Liturgical Press, 1971), 11–18. There are no section numbers or paragraph numbers in this document, so page numbers from Broderick are cited.

> Everyone knows with certitude that a fearful tempest now torments the Church, and that evils afflict society. For violent enemies of God and men have assaulted and trampled upon the Catholic Church, its salutary doctrine, its venerable power, and the supreme authority of the Apostolic See. They have treated with contempt all sacred things; plundered ecclesiastical goods; harassed in all manner of ways bishops, highly esteemed men dedicated to their sacred ministry, and laymen distinguished for their Catholic dispositions; suppressed religious orders and congregations; widely circulated infamous books of all kinds, harmful periodicals, and pernicious sects of various types; taken from the hands of the clergy almost everywhere the education of unfortunate young folk; and what is still worse, entrusted this education in not a few places to teachers of harmful error. (AP, 13)

The negative assessment of the historical climate and numerous descriptions of its assaults on the church indicates that the council's purpose would not be to evaluate modern claims and discern the appropriate stance toward them; instead, it would demonstrate the limitations of the modern worldview and the church's capacity to overcome it.

The pessimistic description of the modern world stands in contrast to the text's certitude in the church's ability to persevere despite this adverse climate. What stands at the center of *Aeterni Patris*'s confidence is the concluding scene of Matthew's Gospel, where Christ leaves his disciples but first promises, "And behold, I am with you until the end of the age" (Matt 28:20). The opening of the letter refers explicitly to this scene:

> After He overcame death, but before He ascended into triumph in heaven to sit at the right hand of the Father, He sent Apostles into the whole world to preach the Gospel to every creature. To them He gave power to rule the Church, which He purchased with His blood, and which He founded as the safe road to salvation, and enriched with heavenly treasures. . . . In order that the government of the same Church might proceed in proper and orderly fashion, and in order that every Christian might continue always in one faith, one charity, and one communion, *He promised to be close at hand always until the end of the world*. (AP, 11–12, emphasis added)

Direct references to Scripture in this letter are rare. Even in the account of Christ's life, described in the document's opening section, only a general summary is included with little direct quotation from the gospels. As such, the multiple allusions to Christ's promise in Matthew 28:20 stand out as conveying a point of particular emphasis. The reason that the apostles, and their successors, can proclaim the Good News and advance the mission of the church is that they are strengthened by the Lord's promise to "be close at hand until the end of the world" (AP, 12). Christ's followers need not fear their own unworthiness or lack of understanding because they know that the Lord will not let them stray too far from God's will. The promise of Christ's presence ensures that the Spirit of truth will always prevail in the church while preserving those who lead it from the danger of error. This guarantee means that the church can offer precisely that which modern society lacks: a principle of authority that provides reliable access to truth and a guarantee of stability.

Christ's perennial presence within the church allows it to serve as "the column and chief support of truth" and that which "displays the light of true doctrine to all peoples" (AP, 11). It is thus able to refute the relativistic claims of the modern world and provide the antidote to the instability which plagues it. In fact, *Aeterni Patris* is explicit that Christ's presence is promised to his disciples for this exact purpose. This is clear in the text's assertion that "in order that the government of the same church might proceed in proper and orderly fashion, and in order that every Christian people might continue always in one faith, one doctrine, one charity, and one communion, He promised to be close at hand always until the end of the world" (AP, 12). Thus, *Aeterni Patris*'s central argument is grounded in its use of Mathew 28:20. While the rationalist worldview advanced the idea that no legitimate authority exists apart from human reason and that knowledge of the supernatural realm, if it in fact exists, is largely inaccessible, *Aeterni Patris* asserts that the supernatural order does exist and that human beings have reliable access to it through the church. This assurance means that men and women can move beyond their anxiety about the volatility of the times and trust the church's ability to lead them to peace and, ultimately, salvation.

Another key dimension of *Aeterni Patris* and its reliance on Matthew 28:20 is its emphasis on the pope's function in exercising the gift promised by Christ. The text highlights Peter's special role as the one chosen by Christ to be "leader of the Apostles, His vicar here on earth, and the head, foundation, and center of the Church; so that with gradation of rank and of honor, and with amplitude of the principle and fullest authority, power and jurisdiction" (AP, 12). He is the one selected to be "the doorkeeper of heaven and judge of what is to be bound and loosed, whose judgments shall retain their validity in heaven" (AP, 12). Thus, the text presents Peter as wielding a power which derives from Christ's promise to the whole church. It is significant to underscore that while *Aeterni Patris* makes a strong connection between Christ's promise and the pope's ability to exercise this gift, Matthew 28:20 itself makes no such connection. The biblical text does not associate this promise with Peter in any way. The link between the pope and Christ's promise is emphasized in *Aeterni Patris* in order to demonstrate that the church not only possesses an inviable principle of authority but also has an irrefutable means of exercising it.

Aeterni Patris provides a glimpse of the strategy that Vatican I will employ to neutralize the threats facing the church. In an effort to address modernity on its own terms, the key theme in the document is authority. Utilizing the resources at its disposal, *Aeterni Patris* treats this locus not in terms of temporal power but in terms of spiritual power. Faced with diminished political and social resources, the church in *Aeterni Patris* leverages its spiritual assets, particularly as a guarantee of its authority to teach effectively. *Aeterni Patris* foreshadows the council's assertion that the church possesses a principle of authority, lacking in modern society, which provides reliable access to truth and a guarantee of stability: Christ's constitutive presence in the church.

IV. *Why* Was Vatican I Called?

Critical to understanding Vatican I is appreciating *why* the council was called. The answer is by no means singular. In the nineteenth century, Rome experienced itself as threatened by multiple traumatic forces. Developments in the ecclesial, political, and philosophical spheres worked independently and collectively to challenge the church's authority and, indeed, its very identity. As a result, Rome adopted an increasingly defensive posture which significantly influenced its self-understanding and sense of its relationship to the world. While theological issues were a contributor to Rome's anxiety, they were certainly not its only source. Any sense that Vatican I grew out of a unanimous conviction that papal infallibility was a burning theological question or that it had surfaced as a clear and organic theological development fails to account for key aspects of the council's context. Presuming that *why* Vatican I was called was solely to provide theological clarity on the topic of papal infallibility leads to a serious misinterpretation of its documents.

The principle purpose of Vatican I was to preserve the independence of the church by securing its voice in a world that seemed, in many ways, increasingly opposed to its very existence. This required engaging internal challenges such as conciliarism and Gallicanism that appeared to inhibit the church's ability to conduct its own affairs and responding to external challenges such as the advent of rationalism and the encroachment of secular powers. The cumulative effects of these external and internal challenges necessitated that the church determine how it would respond to the swiftly emerging new world order. Given its diminished position in the world, the question before Vatican I was how the ecclesial community could preserve its ability to teach and act independently. As Schatz puts it, the issue before the council fathers was whether the church would "locate itself primarily beneath the standard of a fixed and unchangeable authority or present itself more as a historical reality also subject to history and even to change."[31] This was, according to Joseph Burgess, "the question of questions" at the council.[32] As we will see later, understanding *why* Vatican I was called and *why* it taught as it did sheds significant light on *what* the council taught and *how* it taught it.

---

[31] Schatz, *Papal Primacy*, 156.
[32] Burgess, "The Historical Background of Vatican I," 294.

CHAPTER THREE

Vatican I and Its Definition of Papal Infallibility

By one of the leading spirits of the Council it has been emphatically denied that "its object was to define the infallibility of the pope." And justly; for the definition of infallibility was obviously not so much an end, but a means to an end.[1]

—Archbishop Peter Kenrick

Given the consensus regarding the urgency of the contemporary situation and the sense that a strong demonstration of authority was needed to preserve the church's independence, many people presumed that Vatican I would act quickly when it opened on December 8, 1869.[2] Several bishops compared the council's likely

---

[1] Kenrick, *An Inside View of the Vatican Council*, 14.

[2] The urgency of the church's situation was again reiterated in Pius's Opening Allocution at the council's first session. The Allocution reads, in part, "You behold, venerable brothers, the fury with which the ancient enemy of the human race has attacked and still attacks the house of God, where holiness is befitting. He is the promoter of that widespread conspiracy of evil men, which is closely united, richly endowed and supported by institutions. Using freedom as a cloak for malice, this conspiracy wages unceasingly against Christ's holy Church fierce warfare, tainted with crimes of all sorts. You are not unaware of this manner of warfare, its force, its arms, its progress, and its aims. Continually before your eyes are disorder and confusion concerning the sound doctrines on which depends the proper ordering of human affairs; lamentable perversion of every law; and the manifold artifices of audacious lying and corruption, which break the

speed and importance to the historic gathering at Chalcedon in 451, which had served as a turning point in Christian history and lasted less than a month. In the five years intervening between the pope's public suggestion of a council and its opening, there had been considerable movement toward the idea that defining papal infallibility was the only suitable remedy for the errors of the day.[3] The question of whether or not papal infallibility would be defined came to be regarded as simply "the question," and the issue of how it would be treated was debated throughout Europe. The topic sparked such intense interest that Émile Ollivier, author of an important contemporary account of Vatican I, observed that discussions on this matter "began in the market-place, and every one took part, even society ladies between the acts at the Opera."[4] As a result, a rumor began to circulate that, once the council opened, papal infallibility would immediately pass by acclamation. One supporter of this scenario, Archbishop Fabio Chigi, papal nuncio in Paris, hoped that "a unanimous outburst of the Holy Spirit would define it by acclamation by the mouth of the Fathers."[5] Odo Russell, who served as England's unofficial agent at the Vatican during this time, noted in a letter to Cardinal Antonelli in April 1869 that "the tone in which the Cardinals and others speak leads me to think that in the opening ceremony of the Council, the Infal-

---

salutary bonds of justice, integrity, and authority; inflame the basest desires; and root out completely from souls their Christian faith." See "Opening Allocution of Pope Pius IX at the first session of Vatican Council I," in Broderick, *Documents of Vatican I*, 28.

[3] An authoritative study of the emergence of papal infallibility as the best response to the challenges of the day is found in Roger Aubert, "*Les progrès de l'Ultramontanisme*," in his *Le pontificat de Pie IX*, 262–310. Also notable are Butler's two chapters "Ultramontanism," and "The New Ultramontanism," in *Vatican I*, 1:35–56 and 1:57–80. Other important sources on this topic are Hermann Pottmeyer, *Unfehlbarkeit und Souveränität: Die päpstliche Unfehlbarkeit im System der ultramontanen Ekklesiologie des 19. Jahrhunderts* (Mainz: Grünewald, 1975); and Frank Costigan, *The Consensus of the Church and Papal Infallibility: A Study in the Background of Vatican I* (Washington, DC: The Catholic University of America Press, 2005).

[4] Émile Ollivier, *L'Église et l'État au Concile du Vatican*, vol. 1 (Ann Arbor, MI: University of Michigan Library Press, 2010), 57.

[5] See Butler, *The Vatican Council*, 1:109.

libility will be laid down as a *fait accompli* and the Bishops will find themselves assenting to it by their presence in Rome."[6] As such, increasing focus on the *en vogue* matter of "the question" usurped the rightful place of other, more pressing, issues related to the church's nature and relation to the world.

When the bishops finally gathered in St. Peter's on December 8, the feast of the Immaculate Conception, however, they did not call for a definition of papal infallibility by universal acclaim, nor was there a quick movement to define any particular teaching. In fact, no single decree was enacted by the council until more than three months later on March 18. A young participant at Vatican I recounted that "at first it was thought that the opposition would not last long—and our Roman College professors had drawn up decrees which were to be passed in time for the Great Festival of the Epiphany, 1870. It was not to be. . . . The Epiphany came; St. Peter's was crowded, but, instead of decrees new-minted, came an act of faith in the ancient creed."[7] The surprisingly slower and more deliberate pace of the council alerted many to the likelihood that its proceedings, and thus the formulation of a response to contemporary challenges, might be more complicated than had been assumed.

While interest in "the question" had been mounting in the months leading up to Vatican I, the official plan devised by the council's Central Commission was for the gathering to develop a comprehensive document on church. Given the church's lack of resources in the temporal realm, the intention was to respond to the challenges it faced by defining and asserting itself theologically and dogmatically. Thus, the plan was that the council would demonstrate the church's ability to overcome modern assaults by highlighting elements inherent to the church itself. To this end, a schema on the church was produced titled: *Schema constitutionis dogmaticae de ecclesia Christi*.[8] The text consisted of fifteen chapters,

---

[6] See Cwiekowski, *The English Bishops and the First Vatican Council*, 89.

[7] William Barry, *Memories and Opinions* (London: Putnam, 1926), 92.

[8] For a copy of this text with helpful commentary, see Fidelis van der Horst, *Das Schema über die Kirche auf dem I Vatikanischen Konzil* (hereafter *De Ecclesia*) (Paderborn: Verlag Bonifacius-Druckerei, 1963).

none of which were dedicated to the issue of papal infallibility; the church's infallibility was addressed, however, in the ninth chapter, and the eleventh chapter focused on papal primacy. This schema, succinctly known as *De Ecclesia*, sought to address the church in a comprehensive manner, treating the pope's authority as one issue within that larger framework.

Despite the desire to approach the church in a holistic way, soon after the council's opening it became clear that this plan would need to be adjusted. In the fall of 1869, the outbreak of military conflict in Rome grew inevitable as Italian forces neared the city. Given that the council was unlikely to complete its entire program of work, some bishops advocated moving consideration of papal authority to the forefront of the conciliar agenda. Petitions to this effect circulated, asking that the debate on the papacy be scheduled to begin immediately following the discussions on the schema on faith (*De Fide*), thus bypassing the earlier chapters of *De Ecclesia*. Proponents of this revised ordering argued that this strategy would guarantee that the matter which was widely considered the most urgent would be resolved before the council was forced to close. Affirming the pope's power and defining his ability to teach infallibly would capacitate the church to protect itself from dangerous assaults until such a time when the bishops could reconvene. Another argument for this change was based on the gathering's internal dynamics. Some claimed that in light of the way that papal infallibility had come to dominate discussions outside of the council hall, the bishops would be distracted and unable to focus on the other topics until "the question" was put to rest.

A small group of bishops opposed altering the council's agenda in this way, fearing that a disconnected focus on papal authority was inconsistent with the church's tradition. They worried that an isolated, and thus potentially artificial, treatment of this issue could never produce an adequate formulation of the church's belief. They advocated maintaining the original plan of considering the church in a more comprehensive manner, even if this meant that deliberation on some themes would be postponed. Eventually, Pius IX intervened, and on April 29 it was announced that the discussion on the Roman Pontiff's primacy and infallibility would be moved to the beginning of the debate on the schema *De Ecclesia*.

While many were pleased with this decision, seventy-one bishops gathered and submitted a protest stating that this ordering was "against procedure" and "illogical."[9] Thus, prior to any formal debate on this topic, some were concerned that the council's treatment of papal authority was burdened with limiting, if not distorting, factors even before it even reached the council floor.

I. Multiple Approaches to "The Question"

As formal deliberations on *De Ecclesia* began on May 14, 1870, the bishops' opinions regarding the possibility of defining papal infallibility fell into two camps: a majority comprised of approximately eighty percent of the bishops who supported the proposed definition and a minority comprised of the remaining twenty percent who opposed it. While the bishops are generally categorized as being in the majority or minority, depending on whether or not they favored defining the pope's infallibility, important differences distinguish members within these groups. Of particular significance is a division within the majority. Among those bishops who supported a definition, there was a small fraction who desired a maximal articulation of papal power. This group, known as the maximalists or the extreme infallibilists, was made up of very few council fathers, yet their extreme views had a decisive effect on the council's deliberations and ultimately its interpretation.

The maximalist bishops advocated an unlimited view of papal infallibility. They rooted their position not primarily in Scripture or tradition but in the conviction that Christ would necessarily endow his church with the best possible form of governance.[10] In their estimation, no Christian could doubt that the supremely wise and benevolent Christ would choose for his church a structure and exercise of authority that was the best and most useful. An ideal government would inevitably include a clear judge who is

---

[9] Margaret O'Gara includes an account of this protest in her important book *Triumph in Defeat: Infallibility, Vatican I and the French Minority Bishops* (Washington, DC: The Catholic University of America Press, 1988), 117–41.

[10] See Costigan, *Consensus of the Church*, 35–62.

unconditionally reliable and capable of arriving at definitive solutions, and so they reasoned that the Lord would necessarily endow the church with such a figure. This authority, they believed, had been given to Peter and his successors in the promises made to Peter in the gospels (Matt 16:17-19; John 21:15-19). Accordingly, they viewed any rejection or limitation of the pope's ability to teach without error as amounting to a denial of either Christ's power or his trustworthiness. In their mind-set, the power and reliability of Christ's assurances to Peter are so formidable that the proper ordering and function of all the other elements in the church could be deduced from them. In fact, so central were these promises in the eyes of the maximalists that they saw the pope's infallibility as the source of the church's infallibility.

The maximalists believed that in order to convey appropriate trust in the pope's authority and Christ's fidelity to his church, papal power had to be stated in the strongest possible terms. Thus, this group rejected any requirement that the pope needed to rely on the bishops or any factors outside of the Petrine promises to exercise his teaching authority. For them, the certitude and irreformability of an infallible statement came from a divine privilege conferred on the pope and not from the consensus and reception of the church. These extreme infallibilist bishops, relying on the work of Robert Bellarmine, pointed out that it was to Peter and not to a council that Christ said, "Feed my sheep," for Christ "called Peter alone the rock and the foundation, not Peter and a council. From this, it is apparent that all the firmness of legitimate councils comes from the pontiff, not partly from the pontiff and partly from a council."[11] They advocated a notion of papal infallibility as personal, absolute, and separate. They saw the pope's power as personal in that it depended on the will of the pope alone, absolute in that it could not be limited by any conditions, and separate in that it did not rely on any formal consultation. From the maximalists' perspective, one could not accept that God gives the church the papacy to promote unity and truth and then not also believe that God endows the church with the instruments

---

[11] Robert Bellarmine, *Opera Omnia*, vol. 2, ed. Justin Fevre (Frankfurt: Minerva, 1965), 84.

necessary to achieve this end. In the words of Pietro Ballerini, it would have done no good to give Peter the role of merely representing unity "if the force of compelling to unity had not been added to it."[12]

Most members of the majority were not, however, so extreme in their views. The majority of the majority, or the "center group" as they are identified by Francis Sullivan, SJ, supported a definition of the pope's infallibility out of a sense that it provided the most strategic and effective response to contemporary challenges.[13] What interested these bishops, primarily, were sociopolitical issues regarding the reconstruction of the political-social order and the church's place within it. They believed that asserting the pope's ability to teach without error would equip the church to refute modern society's destructive tendencies and promote much-needed stability in the world. Members of the center party saw defining papal infallibility not as a theological priority but as a strategic move necessary for preserving the pope's authority and his ability to protect the church. Thus the members of this group sought to capacitate the pope, on behalf of the entire ecclesial community, to act quickly and decisively when the church's interests were threatened. This would demonstrate the church's possession of and access to a reliable principle of authority, the absence of which was the cause of so many problems plaguing the modern world. The bishops of the center group were not unaware of the potential theological problems with the proposed definition, but they felt that the theological concerns could be dealt with outside of the actual text. They argued that certain complicated aspects of the church's faith could be understood internally by the faithful and did not need to be expressed in the formal definition where the church's opponents would seek to capitalize on every loophole. Thus, while the center group and the maximalists together comprised the majority party at Vatican I, their approaches to papal infallibility were considerably different.

[12] Pietro Ballerini, *De vi ac ratione primatus romanorum pontificum, et de infallibitate in definiendis fidei* (Verona, 1766), 44.

[13] Francis Sullivan, "The Meaning of Conciliar Dogmas," in *The Convergence of Theology: A Festschrift Honoring Gerald O'Collins, SJ*, ed. Daniel Kendall and Stephen Davis (New York: Paulist Press, 2001), 73–86, at 74.

A minority of the bishops at Vatican I opposed the proposed definition of papal infallibility. The primary argument of this group was that presenting the pope's authority as separate from the church's authority by asserting his ability to teach infallibly without need of consulting the bishops was inconsistent with the patrimony of the ancient church. Such a separation gave the impression that it was the pope, not Christ, who served as the principle of the church's unity. The minority viewed the maximalists' position as an innovation created by these bishops to achieve their own ends. The fear of this group was that in formulating an extreme reaction to an extreme threat the church was opening itself up to an even greater problem—distancing itself from its own universal tradition.

The minority agreed that Christ had endowed his church with a reliable source of truth and the ability to eliminate controversy, yet they saw this power rooted in the shared authority of the pope and the bishops. They argued that the faith of the church and its enduring witness does not stand or fall on the decisions of one person; rather, it persists in the presence of the Holy Spirit dwelling throughout the whole community and is made manifest in the consent of the universal church. Even with this conviction, most in the minority were not opposed to asserting that the pope enjoys some form of infallibility. They were willing to affirm an expression of the pope's ability to teach without error as long as it included an acknowledgment that the Roman pontiff employs this prerogative while relying on the witness of the whole church. Leaders of this group suggested a definition of infallibility that followed the formula of St. Antonius which stated that "the pope is not infallible when he acts as an individual and on his own initiative, but he is when he makes use of the advice and the help of the entire church."[14] Such a formulation would ensure that the pope could effectively defend the church but avoid the dangers inherent to deviating from the church's tradition.

The minority also worried that a strong definition of papal authority would exacerbate the already strained relations between

[14] Pottmeyer, *Towards a Papacy in Communion*, 83.

the church and the world. They cautioned that asserting precisely the type of authority against which the modern world was actively defining itself would only further marginalize the church's voice. Such a response could not only elicit external repercussions but also had the potential to incite serious internal problems by polarizing those in the church who wanted to engage modern ideas and those who sought distance from modernity's corruption. Additionally, debating this issue in a conciliar forum would call attention to divisions among the faithful and highlight the existence of dissent within the church at a time when what was needed were demonstrations of unity. There was also concern among some that a formal definition of papal infallibility would have disastrous consequences for relations with Protestants and deter those considering converting to the Catholic faith.[15] Ultimately, the minority felt that the church could better respond to the present crisis by seeking reconciliation, rather than distance. They worried that defining papal infallibility would antagonize the world and further diminish the church's ability to speak meaningfully in the modern world and advance its own mission.

Like the majority, the minority was also not monolithic in its thinking. Among those who opposed defining papal infallibility were some who objected not on theological grounds but on the grounds that they considered the timing inopportune. The reservations of these "inopportunists" can be summarized in terms of four basic concerns: (1) that papal infallibility did not reflect the belief of the faithful; (2) that there was no necessity in defining it; (3) that it would unnecessarily antagonize government leaders; and (4) that it presented problems for ecumenical advance.[16] Many

[15] Some of those separated from Rome expressed hope that the upcoming council would promote unity not only with the world but also with other Christians. In a letter in the *Tablet*, a Dutch Jansenist priest is quoted as saying, "We universally and ardently desire that the Council should put an end to the separation which exists between us and our brethren of the Holy Church. If even the prospect of the Council awakens such desires, what may we not hope from its actual labors?" The *Tablet* (December 5, 1868).

[16] The impact of a formal definition of papal infallibility on potential Protestant converts to Catholicism was a hotly debated topic. Many, including John Henry Newman, believed that any definition of the pope's infallible teaching authority

in this group thought that affirming papal infallibility might be theologically appropriate, yet they wanted to delay a formal definition until the future when the climate might be more conducive to its reception and when such a definition would promote the unity it intended rather than serve as a source of fragmentation.

John Henry Newman was among those who felt that a formal definition of papal infallibility in 1870 was inopportune.[17] After much reflection on this issue, Newman wrote privately of his belief that while there was sufficient evidence to hold papal infallibility as a theological opinion, he did not believe that there was sufficient evidence at this point for unconditional assent. In responding to the endless inquiries that he received on this topic he frequently made this distinction. In a letter to his friend Mrs. William Froude, he stated, "I have only an opinion (not faith), that the Pope is infallible," and to Peter Le Page Renouf he admitted, "I hold the Pope's Infallibility, not as a dogma, but as a theological opinion;

---

would surely deter converts and impede efforts at dialogue. In a long letter dated November 21, 1869, Newman wrote, "If anything could throw into confusion, make skeptics, encourage scoffers, and throw back inquirers, it will be the definition of this doctrine." Manning held the opposite position. He believed that given the thirst among men and women for truth and stability, a solid formulation of papal infallibility would encourage conversions. Manning felt strongly that Catholics had to assert their unique identity clearly and decisively to attract those disillusioned by the instability of the world. On this topic Manning wrote, "Nothing would be more useful to bolster the faith of Catholics and to enlighten non-Catholics than to declare the living assistance with which the Church is endowed in guarding the deposit of faith." For more on this debate, see John R. Page's chapter "Can Any Thing I Say Move a Single Bishop?" in *What Will Dr. Newman Do? John Henry Newman and Papal Infallibility, 1865–1875* (Collegeville, MN: Liturgical Press, 1994), 51–125.

[17] Newman exerted a great influence on the council despite the fact that he did not attend it. His presence as an adviser was requested by at least three bishops, but he rejected each of these requests on different grounds, citing at various times his age, lack of a "strong memory for theological passages," and the fact that such a role was "foreign to his talents." While he was not in attendance at the council, his opinion was vigorously sought after in Rome and influenced the positions of many bishops. For more on Newman and Vatican I, see Page, *What Will Dr. Newman Do?*; and Francis Sullivan, "Newman on Infallibility," in *Newman after One Hundred Years*, ed. Ian Kerr and Alan G. Hill (Oxford: Clarendon, 1990), 420–32.

that is not as a certainty, but as a probability."[18] Newman outlined several arguments which he felt justified his holding papal infallibility as a theological opinion. Not surprisingly, he was most convinced by the evidence offered by the historical exercise of papal teaching authority. Newman stated, "The fact that all along for so many centuries the head of the Church and the teacher of the faithful and the Vicar of Christ has been allowed by God to assert virtually his infallibility is a great argument in favor of the validity of this claim."[19] Thus, Newman believed that it was in fact theologically possible to define the pope's infallible teaching authority as a dogma, but he did not believe that the present circumstances were fitting for such a development.[20]

Newman expressed his views regarding why the timing for a definition of papal infallibility was inopportune in a letter to Father Robert Whitty, SJ, the newly appointed Jesuit Provincial of England who was serving as a theological adviser at the council. He wrote:

[18] Page, *What Will Dr. Newman Do?*, 71.

[19] *Letters and Diaries of John Henry Newman*, vol. 25, ed. Charles Stephen Dessain (London: T. Nelson, 1970), 263.

[20] Döllinger, as a prominent voice among the minority, argued that the inopportunist position was faulty both methodologically and theologically. He wrote, "If your objection to the dogma is that it is unsuited for the times, you thereby admit its truth; for if you thought it doubtful and erroneous, you must have opposed the definition on that ground. By not venturing to assail its truth, you deprive your objection to its opportuneness of all its weight, for when was ever a religious truth, on which eternal salvation depends, suppressed on such a ground as this? Does this holding back, inspired by the fear of men, correspond to the ancient spirit and lofty mission of the Church? How many of her doctrines would she have dared to proclaim had she chosen to wait on the approval of the appropriate age? Rather, for that very reason, must religious truths be loudly and emphatically proclaimed, when a contrary position is growing among men, because thereby an insidious heresy is marked out and judged by the supreme authority in the Church. Your plea of inopportuneness is therefore a fresh and urgent ground for adhering firmly to the solemn definition of infallibility by the Church." He goes on to encourage, "instead you should declare what German bishops have said in their pastoral: 'This doctrine possesses none of the requisite conditions of an article of faith; it has no guarantee either in Scripture or Tradition, and no roots in the conscience and religious mind of the Christian world.'" See Döllinger, *Letters from Rome on the Council* (London: Rivingtons, 1870), 45.

> Well then, my thesis is this: you are going too fast at Rome—on this
> I shall have to insist. It is enough for one Pope to have passed one
> doctrine. . . . We do not move at railroad pace in theological matters
> even in the nineteenth century. We must be patient, and that for two
> reasons: first, in order to get at truth ourselves, and next in order to
> carry others with us. The Church moves as a whole; it is not a mere
> philosophy; it is a communion; it not only discovers, but it teaches;
> and it is bound to consult for charity, as well as for faith.[21]

In his letter, Newman holds up the Immaculate Conception as an
example of the proper means of defining dogma by virtue of the
fact that this Marian doctrine was already believed by the faithful
before it was officially promulgated and not the other way around.
He encouraged Whitty, saying, "Think how slowly and cautiously
you proceeded in the definition of the Immaculate Conception,
how many steps were made, how many centuries passed, before
the dogma was ripe; we are not ripe yet for the Pope's Infallibility.
Hardly anyone even murmured at the act of 1854, half the world
is in a fright at the proposed act of 1870."[22] The concern for Newman and other inopportunists was not that defining papal infallibility was theologically problematic; rather, they feared that
defining it at the wrong time would threaten the very truths which
this teaching surely held.

Reaching an adequate interpretation of Vatican I's teachings on
papal infallibility requires an appreciation of the complexity of
the deliberations on this topic. When considering the debates over
this subject, it is critical to distinguish the small group of maximalist voices from the rest of the majority. Setting the maximalists
apart sheds light on the reality that there was a high level of theological consensus among the vast majority of the council fathers.
Both the minority and the center party agreed that the pope is
endowed with some form of infallible teaching authority and that
the exercise of this authority should normally include consultation
with the universal church. Where the two groups diverged was
over how this authority and this consultation could be appropriately expressed within the formal definition.

---

[21] *Letters and Diaries of John Henry Newman*, 25:263.
[22] Ibid.

Given the fundamental agreement between the center party and the minority, one must ask: why did these two groups remain divided? If the minority could have been satisfied at such a relatively low cost by merely affirming something that both groups already believed—that the pope should consult the whole church in defining matters of faith—then why would the center party remain so recalcitrant? The answer to this question is threefold. First, motivated largely by strategic concerns, the main priority of the center party was to equip the church to act quickly and without encumbrance to defend herself against serious attacks. They considered any attempt to fix the conditions of the pope's consultation of the bishops to be cumbersome and therefore dangerous. They disallowed any qualifications in the definition which might "blunt this weapon" at critical moments when the church needed to act expediently and decisively. They feared that requiring collaboration between the pope and the bishops as a condition of rendering an infallible statement could result in a long, interminable process where more bishops, more abbots, more chapters could always be produced who had not yet been consulted or adequately consulted on a particular teaching, thus calling into question its validity. Such restrictions would mean that the church would be burdened with this slow process of deliberation even in times of grave crisis.

Second, the center party's concerns about the dangers associated with the minority's position were rooted in fears that the latter's views aligned too closely with Gallicanism. To some ways of thinking, Gallicanism had caused grave problems for the church by compromising its independence in relation to the state. While explicit support for Gallican ideas had grown increasingly attenuated since the Revolution, fear of this position lingered based on the memory of its destructive power. There was tremendous anxiety that any insistence on the pope's collaboration with the bishops would be understood in the sense of Gallicanism. Many in the majority considered ruling out the Gallican position as a permissible theological opinion to be one of their primary tasks at the council. The bishops of the center party did not see the Gallicanists' position as theologically motivated but as a capitulation to public opinion and the secular spirit of the age. They maintained a sense that belief in the pope's infallibility reflected a "supernatural attitude" while a belief in the necessity of the pope's consultation with the bishops reflected a "secular attitude."[23] In a similar way, the bishops of the center party did not see the minority's opposition to defining papal infallibility as theologically motivated but as a surrender to "liberal" ideas. To the extent that the minority seemed to keep Gallican ideas alive, the majority felt that their position must be resisted.

Finally, the center party refused to compromise with the minority precisely because the latter's resistance seemed to demonstrate a need for exactly the type of power and expediency that the definition provided. This group considered the minority's insistence on spelling out the conditions of the exercise of papal prerogatives to be unreasonable and unnecessary. Their "foot-dragging" on this matter of intense importance provided a perfect illustration of the church's inability to act in its own self-interest if it is bound to consult the bishops as a whole. It was precisely the debate with the minority that radicalized some in the majority to believe that the definition, in order to be effective, must be promulgated without significant limits. Regarding the delays caused by the minority, Manning commented, "The means taken to prevent the definition made the definition inevitable by proving its necessity."[24] On the other side, the minority refused to be bullied by the sheer numbers and aggression of the majority and out of a sincere fear that "the undefined is unlimited."[25] For the minority bishops, the majority's inability to recognize the potential dangers of an unrestricted definition deepened their sense that measures were needed to keep the church from acting rashly and perhaps recklessly in times of crisis. It would seem that the primary motivations of the center and minority parties, legitimate as they were, effectively hardened their mutual opposition, even as their theological positions were relatively close on the question of papal teaching authority. The frustratingly close but divided positions underscore that conciliar debates are not always framed by wholly oppositional positions.

---

[23] See Costigan, *The Consensus of the Church*, 185.
[24] Manning, *True Story of the Vatican Council*, 71.
[25] Butler, *The Vatican Council*, 2:34.

On the contrary, subtle differences—often attentive to context and timing—exercise strong motivations which divide council fathers.

A critical problem for interpreting Vatican I today lies in the fact that while the central party and the minority, in conversation with one another, shaped the definition of papal infallibility—it is the maximalists' position which is most commonly associated in the popular mind with Vatican I's teaching. Unlike most in the majority who supported papal infallibility for strategic reasons, the maximalists employed theological arguments about the source of the pope's infallibility and viewed his power as virtually boundless. While this extreme position was represented by only a small fraction of the council fathers, the general perception of Vatican I's definition of papal infallibility is that it reflects this viewpoint and, as such, is exclusive of other forms of authority in the church. In reality, the maximalist position was soundly rejected by the vast majority of the council fathers. The debates between the maximalists, the center party, and the minority bishops at Vatican I reveal that the bishops' thinking on papal infallibility was neither uniform nor motivated exclusively by theological concerns; instead it was shaped by a myriad of factors, including theological commitments, historical developments, strategic decisions, and logistical realities. Recognizing these elements of Vatican I's context and development are critical to arriving at an appropriate reading of its final texts.

II. Final Voting on *Pastor Aeternus*

The final voting on Vatican I's Constitution on the Church was, in many ways, as dramatic as the debate on it had been. The session on July 18, 1870, began with a formal reading of the final text. Once this concluded, the bishops were presented with the question, "Right Reverend Fathers, do the decrees and canons contained in this Constitution please you?"[26] As the roll call began in which

[26] Ibid., 162.

each bishop would indicate whether he found the document was pleasing ("*placet*") or not pleasing ("*non placet*") a terrible storm raged outside the basilica. A correspondent for London's *Times* reported:

> The storm, which had been threatening all morning, burst now with the utmost violence, and to many a superstitious mind might have conveyed the idea that it was an expression of divine wrath, as "no doubt will be interpreted by numbers," said one officer of the Palatine Guard. And so the "*placets*" of the Fathers struggled through the storm, while the thunder pealed above and the lightning flashed in every window and down through the dome and every smaller cupola, dividing if not absorbing the attention of the crowd. "*Placet*" shouted his Eminence or his Grace, and a loud clap of thunder followed in response, and then the lightning darted about the *baldacchino* and every part of the church and the conciliar hall, as if announcing the response.[27]

Ultimately, there were 533 votes of "*placet*" and 2 votes of "*non placet*." Notably, sixty-one members of the minority left Rome ahead of this session in order to avoid voting against a teaching supported by the pope and their brother bishops. Of the two "*non placet*" votes, one was cast by Bishop Fitzgerald of Little Rock, Arkansas, who throughout the council had expressed concerns about the definition. Upon the conclusion of the voting and the pope's confirmation of the Constitution, however, he approached the papal throne and bowed before Pius with the words: "*Modo credo, sancta Pater*" or "Now I believe, Holy Father."[28]

Following the session, the pope addressed the bishops present. His words provide a good sense of what was on the mind of the council fathers at this critical time. He addressed them, saying:

> This supreme authority of the Roman Pontiff, venerable Brothers, does not oppress but helps, does not destroy but builds up, confirms in dignity, unites in charity, and strengthens and protects the rights of his Brethren the Bishops. Therefore let those who now are judging

---

[27] Thomas Mozley, *Letters from Rome on the Occasion of the Ecumenical Council, 1869–70*, vol. 2 (London: Longmans, Green and Company, 1891).

[28] Butler, *The Vatican Council*, 2:164

in commotion of mind know that the Lord himself is not in commotion. Let them bethink themselves that a few years ago, holding the opposite position, they abounded in Our sense and in the sense of the majority of this great Council; but then they judged in the spirit of a gentle air. Can two opposite consciences exist in judging the same judgment? Surely not. Therefore may God enlighten minds and hearts; and since He alone doeth great wonders, may He enlighten minds and hearts, that all may come to the bosom of their Father, Christ's unworthy Vicar on earth, who loves them and longs to be one with them; and thus being joined together in the bond of love, we may fight battles of the Lord; so that our enemies may not mock at us, but rather may fear, and at length the arms of malice may yield in the view of truth, and all may be able to say with St. Augustine: "Thou hast called me into Thy admirable light, and lo I see." [29]

Notably, at this key moment of affirming the pope's authority, Pius IX's focus was on the dignity of the bishops. He is careful to underscore that the council's work does not present a threat to episcopal authority; on the contrary, the pope underscores that the definition "strengthens and protects the rights of his Brethren bishops." Also interesting is that the pope's words have a decidedly pastoral character and stress that the definition of papal infallibility is not about the pope alone but about providing for the care and unity of the whole church.

Having settled what was considered the most important business of the council, the intention was for the bishops to move on to other parts of the schema, continuing their work until November 11, St. Martin's Day. On July 19, however, the day following the promulgation of *Pastor Aeternus*, war was declared between France and Prussia. The turmoil that ensued hindered the council's ability to function. On September 20, a siege of Rome began and shortly thereafter Italian troops occupied the city. A month later, on October 20, Pius issued his Apostolic Letter suspending the First Vatican Council indefinitely. Therefore, rather than the comprehensive constitution on the nature of the church that had been intended, the council fathers had to be content with a document

---

[29] Ibid., 164–65.

that focused on only one element of this—the character of the pope's authority.

III. What and How *Pastor Aeternus* Teaches

Vatican I's Dogmatic Constitution on the Church, *Pastor Aeternus*, consists of four chapters that treat the following topics: (1) Christ's institution of the primacy in Peter; (2) the perpetuity of that primacy in the ongoing life of the church; (3) the character of this primacy as the highest juridical authority; and (4) the infallibility of the papal magisterium. The first two chapters were generally not considered controversial in that they dealt with matters about which there had long been consensus. The third and fourth chapters served as the source of conflict, since their content broached new and potentially disputed territory. In studies of papal infallibility, significant attention has been paid to these latter chapters and, most especially, to the final chapter's definition of papal infallibility; to achieve an adequate interpretation of *Pastor Aeternus*, however, the constitution must be viewed as a whole.

In reading *Pastor Aeternus* in its entirety and in light of its historical and theological context, one can see that its definition of papal infallibility is quite moderate relative to the demands of the majority and certainly in relation to that of the maximalists. Given the external pressures and traumas explored in chapter 2, as well as the vast numerical advantage of the majority, one might expect Vatican I's definition of papal infallibility to be monarchial in character, presenting this prerogative as absolute, separate, and personal. Instead, *Pastor Aeternus* presents a circumscribed view of the pope's teaching authority. The moderate character of this definition is reflected in four key aspects of the document: (1) its efforts to show continuity with tradition; (2) its assertion that papal primacy is in the service of the church's unity; (3) its construction of clear limits regarding the exercise of this authority; and (4) its inclusion of distinct silences on matters of importance. Recognizing the existence of these four elements in *Pastor Aeternus* illumines that the extreme interpretations of the text which may seem unavoidable in a cursory reading are, in fact, inaccurate and contrary to the bishops' intentions.

A critical source for appreciating the moderating factors in *Pastor Aeternus* and understanding the intention of the fathers at Vatican I comes from Bishop Vincent Gasser of Austria. At the time of the council, Gasser served as the spokesperson for the *Deputation de Fide* and was charged with the task of gaining support from the minority bishops by demonstrating how the *Deputation* had accommodated their concerns. Prior to the provisional vote on *Pastor Aeternus*, Gasser addressed the council fathers for nearly three hours—meticulously covering key elements of the text and its interpretation. His *relatio* provides what is widely considered the most authoritative interpretation of *Pastor Aeternus*.[30] In fact, Gasser's text is considered so important that Vatican II often cites it, rather than *Pastor Aeternus* itself, as a way of illumining Vatican I's positions and underscoring areas of continuity between the two councils.

The first aspect of *Pastor Aeternus*'s moderate character is reflected in its efforts to situate its definition of papal infallibility within the church's universal tradition. When the decision was made to consider the pope's teaching authority ahead of the other proposed chapters of the schema *De Ecclesia*, many bishops noted that such a consideration posed significant problems. In order to ameliorate these concerns, concerted efforts were made to provide some level of contextualization within the document itself. Accordingly, references from previous councils such as the Fourth Council of Constantinople, the Second Council of Lyons, and the Council of Florence were included to demonstrate that the text's presentation of papal authority is the same as what other ecumenical councils have "always maintained" and what has been "demonstrated in the constant custom of the church" (PA 4).[31]

---

[30] See: *The Gift of the Infallibility: The Official Relatio on Infallibility of Bishop Vincent Gasser at Vatican Council I*, ed. James O'Connor (Boston: St. Paul Editions, 1986).

[31] All quotes from *Pastor Aeternus* are taken from *Decrees of the Ecumenical Councils*, vol. 2, *Trent to Vatican II*, ed. Norman Tanner (Washington, DC: Sheed and Ward, 1990).

Another way that *Pastor Aeternus* roots itself in the Christian tradition is by maintaining the traditional understanding of papal power as protective and conservative rather than creative or innovative. The text rejects any sense that papal infallibility is of a miraculous character or represents a form of divine revelation; instead, it affirms the pope's ability to teach without error as an instance of special guidance by the Holy Spirit. This promise of guidance is given to Peter and his successors not so that they might "make known some new doctrine" but that they might "religiously guard and faithfully expound the revelation or deposit of faith transmitted by the apostles" (PA 4). The protective and conservative character of papal infallibility means that the pope's infallible teaching authority does not separate him from the rest of the church but unites him to the faithful in a special way in that his ability to teach without error exists as the product of his ability to discern the witness of the faithful. The fact that this gift is exercised within a wide context is clearly expressed in the text:

> The Roman Pontiffs, too, as the circumstances of the time or the state of affairs suggested, sometimes by summoning ecumenical councils or consulting the opinion of Churches scattered throughout the world, sometimes by special synods, sometimes taking advantage of other useful means afforded by divine providence, defined as doctrines to be held those things which, by God's help, they knew to be in keeping with sacred scripture and the apostolic traditions. (PA 4)

By demonstrating its consistency with the church's universal tradition and deep connection with the ecclesial community, *Pastor Aeternus* argues that its definition of papal infallibility is not an innovation but merely an affirmation of the ancient practice of acknowledging Rome as a unique witness to the truth of what Christ has revealed to the whole church.

A second moderating feature in *Pastor Aeternus* is found in the way the text presents papal infallibility in the service of the larger cause of the church's unity. This purpose is made explicit immediately in the prologue which states, "In order, then, that the episcopal office should be one and undivided and that, by the union of the clergy, the whole multitude of believers should be held together in unity of faith and communion, he set blessed Peter over the rest of the apostles and instituted in him the permanent principle of both unities and their visible foundation." *Pastor Aeternus* is clear that the unity which papal infallibility promotes is twofold. On one level, the pope's infallibility strengthens the bonds of communion among the episcopate. The text rejects any sense that this power given to Peter's successor diminishes or competes with the bishops' power. Instead, it takes great care in insisting that this gift is a means of strengthening and supporting the episcopate in their ministry. In a critical passage the text states:

> This power of the supreme pontiff by no means detracts from that ordinary and immediate power of episcopal jurisdiction, by which bishops, who have succeeded to the place of the apostles by appointment of the holy Spirit, tend and govern individually the particular flocks which have been assigned to them. On the contrary, this power of theirs is asserted, supported and defended by the supreme and universal pastor; for St. Gregory the Great says: "My honour is the honour of the whole church. My honour is the steadfast strength of my brethren. Then do I receive true honour, when it is denied to none of those to whom honour is due." (PA 3)[32]

On a second level, by building communion among the bishops, papal infallibility also promotes union among all the faithful. *Pastor Aeternus* argues that the pope's ability to teach without error unites the bishops in love and truth; this unity among the episcopate, in turn, fosters authentic faith and communion among the faithful.[33] It is ultimately through their union with the Roman pontiff and in profession of the same faith, that "the Church of Christ becomes one flock under one supreme shepherd" (PA 3). By emphasizing the Petrine ministry as a service of unity—and papal infallibility as an instrument of this service—*Pastor Aeternus*

---

[32] Pottmeyer notes that this paragraph, emphasizing that the primacy is not a threat to the ordinary and immediate jurisdiction of the bishops, represents the most important achievement of the minority bishops at Vatican I. See Pottmeyer, "Recent Discussions on Primacy in Relation to Vatican I," in *The Petrine Ministry*, 210–30, at 223.

[33] See Michael J. Buckley, *Papal Primacy and the Episcopate: Towards a Relational Understanding* (New York: Herder and Herder, 1998), 49.

roots its teachings on the power's authority not in a notion of power but in the pope's fundamental responsibility to promote unity and build relationships within the body of Christ. The text is clear that the papacy is constituted in these relationships and has its term in them.[34] Thus, just as the council fathers sought to contextualize papal infallibility within the church's tradition they also sought to contextualize it within a wider ecclesiology which considers the church as a whole.

Pastor Aeternus makes significant use of Matthew 28:20 and the idea of Christ's enduring presence in the church just as in Pius IX's encyclical *Aeterni patris*. The title of the Constitution itself—*Pastor Aeternus,* or Eternal Shepherd—reflects the fact that Christ's constant presence guiding and protecting the church serves as a central theme in the text. *Pastor Aeternus* begins by stating that it was the Lord's desire to "build a church in which, as in the house of the living God, all the faithful should be linked by one faith and one charity" (PA, Prologue). In order to achieve this end, "It was his will that in his church there should be shepherds and teachers until the end of time" (PA, Prologue). Thus, it is out of a desire to safeguard his church that Christ remains within it and capacitates some for leadership. Accordingly, papal infallibility is presented as a gift "which the divine Redeemer willed his church to enjoy" and not a power given to the pope individually (PA 4). *Pastor Aeternus*'s reliance on Mathew 28:20 and the concept of Christ as eternal shepherd demonstrates a close relationship between Christ and the church and it is this closeness which is represented in the pope's infallible teaching authority.

A third aspect of moderation in *Pastor Aeternus* is the existence of clear limits in the pope's exercise of his infallible authority. Gasser dedicates a significant portion of his *relatio* to demonstrating that the proposed definition does not depict the pope's authority in the extreme way that the maximalists desired. He begins by noting that God's infallibility alone is absolute, and therefore, all other forms must have limits. On this point he writes:

[34] Ibid.

> Absolute infallibility belongs only to God, the first and essential
> truth who can never deceive or be deceived in any way. All other
> infallibility, by the fact that it is communicated for a certain end, has
> limits and conditions by which it is judged to be present. This is also
> true of the infallibility of the Roman Pontiff.[35]

Gasser is careful to describe three distinct ways in which the
pope's infallibility is limited—in relation to its *object*, its *active
subject*, and its *act*. In regard to the *object* of infallible teachings,
the pope's prerogative is explicitly restricted to instances where
he "defines a doctrine of faith and morals" (PA 4). The text is clear
that the guarantee of infallibility does not apply to the pontiff's
every act or utterance but is in effect only when he defines a teaching that is part of the apostolic tradition and the common faith of
the church.

The pope's teaching authority, Gasser points out, is also limited
in relation to its *active subject*. The pope enjoys the gift of infallibility exclusively in instances when he teaches "in his office as teacher
and shepherd of Christians" (PA 4). While it is true that papal
teaching authority is, in some sense, personal in that it is tied to
the person of the pope as Peter's successor, it is clear that this
power is not at the disposal of a private individual. This prerogative is not a personal possession but an authority exercised by the
pope on behalf of the church as a privilege which "the Divine
Redeemer willed for his Church to enjoy" (PA 4). The pope, even
as officeholder of the papacy, nevertheless acts, at times, outside
of his universal office. For example, he may speak authoritatively
but in the limited office of Bishop of Rome to those in his diocese;
other times he may speak as an individual pastor, say in a discrete
homily or in local public remarks; and finally, he may sometimes
act as a purely private individual who speaks about a point of
faith or morals. Ultimately, it is by virtue of his relationship to the
whole church that the pope is able to teach without error; apart
from this relationship he does not enjoy the same prerogative.

Finally, Gasser affirms that the gift of infallibility given to the
pope is restricted in relation to its *act*. Infallible teachings must be

---

[35] Gasser, *The Gift of Infallibility*, 45.

made *ex cathedra* where the pope expressly declares that what is being defined represents a definitive judgment which the entire church is obliged to hold. The pope's ability to teach infallibly is separate from the teachings that he presents as the leader of the church but which are not meant to be binding on all the faithful. These clear and significant limits guarantee that the pope does not wield his authority without qualification; rather, he is bound to distinct conditions which reflect an understanding that the primary recipient of the gift of infallibility is the entire church.

A fourth moderating element in *Pastor Aeternus* is the existence of key silences in the text. As we have seen, *Pastor Aeternus* is clear that the pope's authority is not competitive with episcopal authority and, in fact, is intended to strengthen and support the bishops in their ministry. After asserting the noncompetitive relationship of the two authorities, however, the document does not elaborate on how these two subjects of power are complementary. Similarly, while *Pastor Aeternus* affirms the authority of the bishop, it is silent on the specific powers granted to the episcopate and the relationship of these powers to those granted to the pope. While some interpreters have maintained that the absence of an explicit affirmation of episcopal authority in *Pastor Aeternus* is a reflection that the council fathers had a weak view of the role of the bishops, in reality the text says very little about the character of the bishops' authority except to say that the pope's authority "by no means detracts" from it (PA 4). Avery Dulles points to the existence of critical silences in the text by observing, "The Fathers at Vatican I were conscious that papal power in the Church was limited, but they were unable, in terms of their own categories, to specify any limiting principle."[36] To put Dulles's point more succinctly, the silences of *Pastor Aeternus* indicate limits without defining them. Therefore, while some argue that *Pastor Aeternus* forbids those rights which it does not include, it is more accurate to grant that issues which Vatican I does not address remain open questions

---

[36] Avery Dulles, *The Catholicity of the Church* (Oxford: Clarendon Press, 1985), 136.

or, as Pottmeyer states, "[O]n those things about which the text is silent, it renders no judgment."[37]

Gasser devotes considerable time in his *relatio* to addressing the question of the relationship between the pope's authority and the bishops' authority. He notes that because the pope's infallibility is not a form of divine revelation, there is certainly a need for the pontiff to consult the whole church and collaborate with the bishops. Speaking on behalf of the Deputation, Gasser affirms this point by saying, "We do not in the least separate the Pope from the consent of the Church, provided that consent be not put as a condition as we believe the Pope to be by divine assistance infallible, we thereby also believe that the assent of the Church can never be wanting in these definitions; as it is not possible that the body of bishops can be separated from their head, nor can the universal church fail."[38] While Gasser is clear that consultation between pope and bishops is a normal and appropriate element within the development of an infallible teaching, he is adamant that neither the necessity nor the means of such a consultation can be fixed in the definition.

Gasser affirms the minority's sense that there is a need, in principle, for the pope to seek the wisdom of the whole church in defining matters to be held by all the faithful, yet he denies that this consultation constitutes a necessary condition of the exercise of this authority. Gasser outlines several reasons why the consent of the bishops is not an essential condition for the exercise of the pope's infallible teaching authority. One of these is that it is possible for the pope to employ other means for determining the faith of the church, such as turning to Scripture or the witness of the early church.[39] He states that consultation between the pope and bishops on the content and opportuneness of particular infallible statements constitutes a "relative necessity" but not an "absolute necessity" and, as such, cannot be established as a rule.[40] Gasser writes:

[37] Pottmeyer, *Towards a Papacy in Communion*, 108.
[38] Quoted in Butler, *The Vatican Council*, 2:136.
[39] Gasser, *The Gift of Infallibility*, 51.
[40] Ibid.

> We are dealing with a strict and absolute necessity of episcopal advice and help in every dogmatic judgment of the Roman Pontiff, so much that it must have its place in every definition of our dogmatic constitution. *It is in this strict and absolute necessity that the whole difference between us consists.* The difference does not consist in the opportuneness or some relative necessity which must be completely left to the judgment of the Roman Pontiff as he determines according to the circumstances. As such, this type of necessity cannot have a place in the definition of a dogmatic constitution.[41]

Gasser suggests that the problem with the minority's position is their insistence on formalizing a condition whereby the pope is obligated to consult the bishops rather than merely affirming the appropriateness of such a consultation. The insistence risks turning what is properly a moral obligation into a juridical condition. Gasser denies the idea that such collaboration is rejected by the definition simply because it is not explicitly stipulated. The fact that consulting the bishops, according to Gasser, exists as a "rule of faith" is affirmed in the text through its moderating features.[42] What Gasser strives to show is that the real differences between the minority and most in the majority are not theological. The differences lie in their understandings of what constitutes an appropriate definition; one could characterize this as a difference in the mode of proclamation and what's needed for its full articulation. These differences regarding the precise formulation of the definition are significant in Gasser's mind, but he also cautions that they should not overshadow the more fundamental theological agreement that exists among the bishops.

Gasser's point about the difference between a moral obligation and a juridical condition also helps to clarify issues related to the most controversial aspect of *Pastor Aeternus,* the *ex sese* clause at the end of the text. This clause was added to the definition of papal infallibility by the Deputation on the Faith very late in the council's deliberations without any debate among the council fathers. Originally, the final sentence of the definition read: "Therefore, such definitions of the Roman Pontiff are therefore irreformable of them-

---

[41] Ibid., 48 (emphasis mine).
[42] Ibid., 50.

selves." The amendment was hastily added "and not because of the consent of the church" (*ex sese, non autem ex consensus Ecclesiae*). While this clause does not substantively alter the meaning of the definition, the way that it amplifies the defensive tone of the text has long been offered as evidence of the rigidity of the definition and the fact that it ascribes a weak role to the episcopate. Gasser, however, clarifies that this clause is meant to be understood juridically and not theologically. The intent of this addition is to make the juridical claim that there is no single person or collective body that wields authority higher than that of the pope; it does not intend to render a theological judgment about the pope's power as separate from that of the church. The fact that the wording of the *ex sese* clause is taken directly from the fourth Gallican article makes it clear that this addition is intended to refute a claim about the exercise of the pope's power and not to convey a theological decision.[43] Thus, understood within its appropriate context, the *ex sese* clause, while it is often viewed as the most problematic element of *Pastor Aeternus*, in fact, provides further evidence that its teachings contain numerous moderating elements that condition the meaning of the text in significant ways.

IV. Conclusion:
Looking at *What* and *How* Vatican I Teaches

Misunderstandings of Vatican I's texts stem, in many ways, from incorrect understandings of *what* the council taught. Typically, if people know anything about Vatican I, it is that it taught that the pope is infallible. While this is true in a particular sense, it is not true in many other senses. People often misunderstand *what* the council taught because they presume that it presents a view of infallibility like that of the maximalists, one where the pope's ability to teach without error has no limits. Thus, many receive

---

[43] Note that the fourth Gallican article reads, "Though the Pope has the chief part in determining questions of faith, and though his decrees have force in the entire Church and in each particular church, yet his decisions are not irreformable, at least until they are approved by the verdict of the entire Church."

the decree on papal infallibility as meaning that the pope can speak on any subject and whatever he says must be held, without question, by all the faithful. This misunderstanding fosters the impression that Vatican I conflicts with modern sensibilities and, as such, contributes in a powerful way to the marginalization of its voice. As we have seen, however, *what* Vatican I teaches regarding the pope's authority is quite circumscribed and subject to several distinct limits and moderating factors. The pope's authority is not presented as *separate* insofar as it is rooted in a gift whose recipient is the entire church; it is not *personal* in that the pontiff exercises it only "in the discharge of his office as shepherd and teacher of all Christians" (PA 4); and it is not *absolute* because it is only in force when the pope defines that a doctrine concerning faith and morals must be held by the whole church. Further, it is not the case that this expression of the pope's authority is exclusive of other forms of ecclesial authority or that it competes with episcopal power. Therefore, a properly contextualized reading shows that *what* Vatican I teaches is a legitimate but limited presentation of one aspect of the pope's authority.

Readers also often misunderstand *what* Vatican I taught by assuming that the definition of papal infallibility is primarily about a particular act of power and the conditions in which it is exercised. Given the general consensus that only a single instance of a pope teaching infallibly has occurred since 1870—the formal definition of the Assumption of Mary by Pius XII in 1950—it would seem that all the energy expended by the council fathers was unnecessary. A true understanding of *what* Vatican I sought to express, however, illumines that the rare exercise of this authority does not call into question its importance or legitimacy. The intent of the majority bishops at Vatican I, the maximalists excluded, was not to define a teaching that would be used regularly but to affirm a close and reliable connection between Christ and the church. Vatican I's definition of papal infallibility is not about an act of power but a relationship between Christ and the church which affords the latter protection, stability, and access to truth. Schatz speaks to this point in asserting that the function of this dogma is not dependent "on whether or how often it was actually put into practice by the issuance of *ex cathedra* definitions in specific matters. It is more a matter of the overall security it gave to the Church gathered around the pope as it pursued its way in the world."[44] The significance of *what* Vatican I taught about papal infallibility is not to be measured in the breadth of this power or in the frequency of its use but in its assertion of a fundamental aspect of the church's identity. Ultimately, *what* Vatican I taught with its definition of papal infallibility is not primarily about the use of a power but about the character of a relationship.

Vatican I is also misunderstood because scholars are not sufficiently sensitive to *how* the council taught. Vatican I was called as a way for the church to respond to what it perceived to be potentially catastrophic threats. These challenges elicited a highly defensive reaction within the church which shaped its approach to the world and the style of its documents. The council's strident tone and negative assessment of the world often alienate contemporary readers and make it difficult for them to see beyond these elements in order to engage the actual theological ideas presented. Another important element of recognizing *how* Vatican I taught is that some of its formulations are meant to be understood in a juridical sense instead of a theological sense. In contrast to the uncertainties of its day, Vatican I sought to provide clear, precise, and unassailable definitions and thus to teach with "the greatest accuracy." The council sought to counter claims that truth is inaccessible and external authority unreliable by asserting that the church's teachings were patent and irrefutable. In this context, the majority bishops were careful to craft the definition of papal infallibility in a way that would allow this authority to be exercised effectively without the threat that technicalities would render it useless. Several of their formulations, chosen for juridical clarity, were mistakenly seen as representing theological commitments. Disagreements and confusion over the genre of particular statements caused problems for the majority and the minority at the time of the council and continues to complicate contemporary efforts to interpret its teachings appropriately today.

---

[44] Schatz, *Papal Primacy*, 165.

A final critical element of *how* Vatican I taught is the recognition that its teachings are incomplete in relation to the council's own goals. The council sought to effectively and definitively respond to the challenges of its day by developing a comprehensive reflection on the nature of the church and its authority but was, due to its untimely prorogation, able to offer only a partial response. In many ways, Vatican I served as an "emergency solution," an attempt by the church to meet the grave challenges of the day with limited time and restricted resources. Many contemporary readers have lost sight of the fact that *Pastor Aeternus* was defined as a remedy for a particular set of concerns and assume that its teachings intend to present the exhaustive word on ecclesial authority, even representing the unanimous view of the bishops who were present. Additionally, readers presume that the council's constitutions are purely theological texts that the bishops composed as complete and totalizing expressions of the faith of the church. This misleading perspective results not only from a forgetfulness created by distance but also by the active efforts of some maximalist interpreters who worked to establish this emergency solution as normative. An appropriately contextualized reading, however, shows that there is significant openness within Vatican I's articulation of papal authority created by distinct limits, important silences, and other moderating elements. Thus, it is not the case that the problem with Vatican I's teachings is that they are wrong so much as that they are particular and limited.

Properly understood, *what* Vatican I taught about papal infallibility need not be understood as inconsistent with Christian tradition or incompatible with modern sensibilities. Rather, it constitutes one legitimate articulation of the church's faith developed in a particular time and place as a way of helping the church preserve its independence and its ability to speak meaningfully to contemporary concerns. Understanding *what* it taught requires appreciating *why* the council was called and *why* the majority of council fathers viewed papal infallibility as the best available remedy for the challenges of its day. Grasping *what* the council taught also involves recognizing *how* it taught—the impact of its tone, genre, and particular perspective. Directing questions of *what*, *why*, and *how* at Vatican I shows that the council is not an outlier in the church's tradition and not necessarily incompatible with contemporary men's and women's self-understanding. Ultimately, a contextualized reading of Vatican I shows that the council's voice is much more moderate than is generally perceived. Moreover, doing so demonstrates that Vatican I does, in fact, have a great deal to contribute in regard to some of the most urgent contemporary questions.

Chapter Four

Is the Council Finished or Unfinished?

Now a distinct promise was given to the bishops that these two points [episcopal authority and the relation between the pope and the bishops] should be treated immediately after the question of the Pope's infalli- bility had been settled. A Roman cardinal told me that he had voted Placet *on the ground of this promise—and other bishops did the same. If the Council had met this winter these subjects would have been treated and now they are only postponed as the Council is only prorogued not closed.*[1]

—Bishop William Clifford

Soon after Vatican I's premature suspension, a controversy sur- faced regarding whether or not the council could be considered finished. To be clear, when the bishops were sent home in 1870, there was no doubt that they had been unable to complete their entire program of work. The council had only been able to address one chapter of the proposed schema on the church and one part of the schema on faith. As time passed, however, discussions arose regarding whether the work that remained was still necessary, given what the council had, in fact, been able to accomplish.

The maximalist bishops were outspoken in their view that the unconsidered aspects of the schema *De Ecclesia* were rendered

---

[1] "Clifford to Bonomi, 17 November, 1870." Included in Cwiekowski, *The En- glish Bishops and the First Vatican Council*, 300.

moot in light of *Pastor Aeternus*'s pronouncement on papal infallibility. These bishops were quick to promote the idea that the council had not only ended conversations regarding papal infallibility but also had effectively concluded all debate on authority in the church. As such, these figures sought to present Vatican I's teachings as "the definitive culmination of ecclesiology and the ecclesiastical order."[2] In many ways, this interpretation was not difficult to promote given what had transpired at the council. The abrupt conclusion of the council's debate on *Pastor Aeternus* led to the perception that the entire discussion on the church and ecclesial authority was over rather than the sense that only one aspect of this conversation had been decided. Now that the pope could teach without error, many reasoned that there was no need to address other issues of ecclesial identity and authority and, perhaps, no need for further councils. The minority advanced the exact opposite position, namely, that treating the rest of the schema was essential to understanding the nature of the church in general and papal infallibility in particular. Therefore, debates ensued regarding whether Vatican I should be considered finished or merely suspended. These exchanges, as we will see, were not trivial or esoteric but crucially important to the council's interpretation.

That Vatican I had definitively resolved issues regarding the pope's authority was not a subject of controversy. The question of papal infallibility was considered exhausted by the minority and majority alike and, thus, rehashing it further was viewed by both parties as neither possible nor desirable. While many minority bishops continued to have serious disagreements with *Pastor Aeternus*'s depiction of papal infallibility, the reality that it had been formally defined and affirmed by a majority of bishops meant that their dissatisfaction could not be expressed by critiquing what the text said but only by focusing on what had been left unsaid. Therefore, upon their return home, the focus of many of the minority bishops shifted from actively critiquing *Pastor Aeternus* to examining the questions left undefined by the council, as these

---

[2] Pottmeyer, *Towards a Papacy in Communion*, 111.

silences seemed to offer the best remedy for addressing the perceived imbalances.[3] As a result, following Vatican I, it was not "the question" of papal infallibility that captured the minority bishops' attention but "the silences" within the definition. The goal of these bishops became keeping these silences and the council's unfinished status alive in the hope that the definition of papal infallibility would ultimately receive proper contextualization.

I. A "Distinct Promise"

At the time of *Pastor Aeternus*'s promulgation, there were hopes, and even assurances, that when the council resumed, the first order of business would be to complete the outstanding aspects of *De Ecclesia*.[4] Foremost on this agenda would be a consideration of the bishops' authority and the relation between their authority and that of the pope. A letter of William Clifford, bishop of Clifton, England, affirms this and provides insight into the tremendous weight placed on this guarantee. In this letter, Clifford notes that many of the minority bishops had voted *placet* to *Pastor Aeternus* on the grounds of "a distinct promise" that the issue of episcopal authority would be treated immediately after the question of papal infallibility had been settled.[5] Their votes had relied on assurances that a more comprehensive discussion of the nature of authority in the church was forthcoming and that these imminent teachings would contextualize the position articulated in the decree in a wider theological context. Clifford's letter illumines the fact that, for many in the minority, it was only the belief that such discussions were merely delayed that had allowed them to consent to what they saw as an incomplete and flawed presentation of ecclesial authority.

---

[3] See O'Gara's masterful treatment of this minority's use of silence in her *Triumph in Defeat*, 175–99.

[4] Butler, *The Vatican Council*, 2:232.

[5] "Clifford to Bonomi, November 17, 1870," in Cwiekowski, *The English Bishops and the First Vatican Council*, 300.

Following the promulgation of *Pastor Aeternus* but before the council's suspension, John Henry Newman contacted Clifford requesting information about the minority bishops' opinion regarding whether matters related to papal infallibility could still be considered unresolved. He was eager to learn whether the minority bishops had "yielded" to the majority's view of the definition or whether there was still a "concerted effort" to stand against it.[6] In a similar letter dated July 27, 1870, he deals with this issue. Regarding the minority's mind-set he writes:

> If they separate and go home without acting as a body, if they act only individually, or as individuals, and each in his own way, then I should not recognize in their opposition to the majority that force, firmness and unity of view which creates a real case of want of moral unanimity in the Council. Again, if the Council continues to sit, if the dissentient Bishops more or less take part in it, and concur in its acts; if there is a new Pope, and he continues on the policy of the present; and if the Council terminates without any reversal or modification of the definition, or any effective movement against it on the part of the dissentients, then again there will be good reason for saying the want of moral unanimity has not been made out.[7]

In Newman's view, if the minority bishops were united in a sustained and legitimate opposition to Vatican I's decree, this would indicate that the church had not yet reached a final decision on this issue. Such a situation would mean that those unhappy with the definition could legitimately dissent from it or withhold their judgment. If, however, *Pastor Aeternus*'s definition of papal infallibility was an unchallenged teaching of the church, then such a

---

[6] "Newman to Clifford, August 12, 1870," in Cwiekowski, *The English Bishops and Vatican I*, 294–95.

[7] This letter is titled by Newman "My formal opinion, Letter 1." Newman marked it "not sent." In this letter he also states, "And further, if the definition is constantly received by the whole body of the faithful, as valid or as the expression of a truth, then too it will claim our assent by the force of the great dictum *securus judicat orbis terrarium*. This indeed is the broad principle by which all acts of the rulers of the Church are ratified." See Cwiekowski, *The English Bishops at Vatican I*, 310. This letter was eventually published as part of his famous work, *A Letter Addressed to His Grace the Duke of Norfolk: On the Occasion of Mr. Gladstone's Recent Expostulation* (London: B. M. Pickering, 1875).

position was not possible. On August 15, 1870, Clifford replied to Newman's inquiry, stating that the matter was still undecided and that, in his mind, this meant that strict adherence to the decree was not obligatory. Clifford is quick to add, however, that the minority's opinion would not impinge on the validity of the definition if it were the case that all the faithful held the definition as a matter of faith. Clifford writes, "Of course, even if the nature of the Council remained doubtful, still if the doctrines taught by it were generally accepted and believed, that would show them to be part of the teaching of the Church, and so the separate infallibility of the Pope would on that ground have to be accepted as of faith. But this also requires time. This is all, I think, I can say at present."[8] With this addendum, Clifford points to another aspect of the definition which remained unsettled: its reception among the faithful. This was another factor that, for many in the minority, slowed the process of discerning the meaning of Vatican I's teaching and the extent to which it could be considered final.[9]

Memories of the "distinct promise" to treat questions related to episcopal authority continued to exert an influence on Vatican I's interpretation even after the council was prorogued in October 1870. Despite the emerging reality that this promise would not be realized any time in the foreseeable future, many in the minority continued to maintain that *Pastor Aeternus* could not be properly interpreted in its present formulation. This view fueled ongoing debates regarding the extent of the pope's responsibility to consult the universal church and the true origin of episcopal authority which were, in many ways, an extension of the debates that had taken place at the council. Regarding the enduring debates, Clifford observes, "The decree does not solve these questions, they may therefore still be considered open. More than this: their right solution must depend on two other questions still pending before the Council, viz. 1st what is 'that infallibility with which the divine Redeemer willed that His Church should be endowed for defining

---

[8] "Clifford to Newman, August 15, 1870," (Archives of the Diocese of Clifton, Letters from William Clifford, Part I). Included in Butler, *The Vatican Council*, 2:177–78.

[9] For more on the reception of Vatican I, see O'Gara, *Triumph in Defeat*, 175–255.

doctrine' and secondly what is the real position of Bishops in the Church."[10] Clifford's words express the sense, held by many, that there were still vital issues pending before the council, issues whose significance was so great that its decrees could not be properly interpreted without their resolution. The sense that the bishops' "real position" was not yet clear was provided as a rationale by the minority for their argument that Vatican I's formulations did not properly express the faith of the church and, as such, were not at present binding.

Many of the minority bishops clung to Vatican I's prorogued status in that they felt it freed them from having to render an evaluation of the council's decrees or support them in their existing form. Some bishops adopted a "posture of waiting" as a means of countering the prevailing maximalist interpretations, noting that commenting on the existing decree would be premature.[11] They hoped that time would "cut down the sharp edges" of the definition so that it could be seen as fitting within a larger framework of ecclesiastical authority.[12] Optimistic members of the minority reasoned that "since *Pastor Aeternus* is binding on our faith . . . its content must be capable of yielding acceptable interpretations."[13] As such, they trusted that time and the guidance of the Spirit would illumine how the teaching could be seen as consistent with Christian tradition. The belief that *Pastor Aeternus* remained unfinished and that, as such, it could not be adequately interpreted was so passionately held among the minority bishops that a meeting of this group came to an informal agreement that *Pastor Aeternus* was "not final"; consequently, the bishops concluded that they would not "try to impose it upon the faithful" unless "some

---

[10] "Clifford to Bonomi, November 17, 1870" (Archives of the Diocese of Clifton, Letters to William Clifford, Part I). Included in Cwiekowski, *The English Bishops and the First Vatican Council*, 300.

[11] This phrase comes from O'Gara from her chapter, "On Material Authority: An Acceptable Interpretation of *Pastor aeternus* Is Possible," in *Triumph in Defeat*, 194–218.

[12] "Vaughan to Maskell, 2 September 1870," in Cwiekowski, *The English Bishops and the First Vatican Council*, 292.

[13] O'Gara, *Triumph in Defeat*, 195.

bull comes from Rome."[14] As Bishop William Vaughn, a participant at the meeting, wrote afterward to a fellow member of the
minority, "If we wait a little we shall have some calm and moderate pastorals, a treatise on the subject. In the meantime let us say:
'I believe what the Church believes, nothing more nor less.'. . .
Let us have patience and all will be well."[15] For some, this posture
was a form of optimism while for others it was more a sign of
resistance. Either way, the minority's silence was intended as a
means of preserving a space so that Vatican I's teachings might
eventually achieve greater balance.

Ultimately, in December 1870, Clifford came to the conclusion
that formal acceptance of *Pastor Aeternus* could no longer be delayed due to pressures from Rome and the needs of his diocese.
When he reached this decision, he again wrote to Newman to
explain why he felt he had to change his position.

> There is now no reasonable prospect of the Bishops meeting again
> in Council for a long time to come; the doctrine has everywhere been
> openly taught without any organized stand having been made
> against it by the Bishops of the minority, several of whom have
> openly expressed their adhesion to it. As to the objections raised
> against the Council itself, they do not seem to me to affect the real
> point in question. In the history of several of the Councils events are
> recorded which we deplore without disputing the conclusions ar-
> rived at. In this case the main fact is indisputed, that the Pope with
> the approval of a large majority of the episcopate has proclaimed a
> certain doctrine, which has been taught throughout the Church
> without any resistance being offered by the bishops who opposed
> it at the Council. Even if opposition were offered by a few bishops,
> this could only result in a schism. The definition therefore must be
> accepted as the voice of the Church and as such, undoubtedly true.[16]

Clifford's words reflect a sentiment that began to grow among the
minority as the council's suspension continued with no end in
sight, namely, that for the health and unity of the church, it was

[14] See Cwiekowski, *The English Bishops and the First Vatican Council*, 286.

[15] "William Vaughan to Maskell, September 11, 1870," in Cwiekowski, *The English Bishops and the First Vatican Council*, 292.

[16] "Clifford to Newman, December 9, 1870," in Cwiekowski, *The English Bishops and the First Vatican Council*, 303.

necessary to let go of the opposition to Vatican I's presentation of papal infallibility. Disputes over this teaching needed to be put to rest, given that their potential to create division and promote instability were greater than what stood to be immediately gained. Such a concession was required, given the tumultuous climate of the day, so that individual dioceses could restore normal order and so that the church might shift its energies to responding to the ongoing problems it faced. Many, like Clifford, hoped that, with time, a deeper understanding of the truth of the definition would come to light, yet they came to the recognition that continuing to call the legitimacy of Vatican I's teaching into question was not the best way to pursue this end.

Newman came to a similar conclusion. He remarked that, in his opinion, it was the case that the definition needed not so much to "be undone as to be completed." [17] To his friends and colleagues who were nervous about a formal definition of papal infallibility, he urged patience and stressed that it was the nature of the Christian community to begin with an idea and perfect it over time. Given the transcendent nature of the truth which dogmatic formulations seek to express, they are not immediately conceived in their fullness; rather, they begin as incomplete expressions of faith that preserve certain truths until they can develop more completely over time. This, he argued, was clearly demonstrated in the church's conciliar tradition which had regularly brought greater clarity and fullness to doctrines formulated by earlier gatherings. Newman wrote:

> Looking at early history, it would seem as if the Church moved on to the perfect truth by various successive declarations, alternately in contrary directions, and thus perfecting, completing, supplying each other. Let us have a little faith in her I say. Pius is not the last

---

[17] Quoted in Ian Kerr, *John Henry Newman: A Biography* (Oxford: Oxford University Press, 1988), 661. For more on Newman and the infallibility question see Kerr's book as well as Paul Misner, *Papacy and Development: Newman and the Primacy of the Pope* (Leiden: E. J. Brill, 1976); Page, *What Will Dr. Newman Do?*; Francis Sullivan, "Newman on Infallibility," in *Newman after One Hundred Years*; and Avery Dulles, "Newman on Infallibility," *Theological Studies* 51 (1990): 434–49.

> of the Popes. The fourth Council modified the third, the fifth the
> fourth. . . . The late definition does not so much need to be undone,
> as to be completed. It needs safeguards to the Pope's possible acts—
> explanations as to the matter and extent of his power. . . . Let us
> be patient, let us have faith, and a new Pope, and a reassembled
> Council may trim the boat.[18]

Newman consistently advised his correspondents not to become
vexed about the definition of papal infallibility; instead he encouraged them to look for the good that it might achieve in its fullness.
In a letter to a Mrs. Helbert, who had written for Newman's coun-
sel on this matter, he recommended that she avoid being overly
anxious; he wrote, "Trust in God, be patient as a duty—*don't give
up what you have*—but pray God to give you all that He has to give,
and to teach you His full will."[19] He assured her that a definition
would serve as neither the last step nor the final word on this
matter. Newman was certain that, in time, the church would come
to the truth of this matter, even if this particular decree did not
convey it completely.

II. Keeping the Questions Alive

The efforts of minority bishops reflect an earnest attempt to
retain the open status of Vatican I's work and its decrees. Moreover, the minority hoped that the existence of distinct silences in
the conciliar texts would create space for complementary positions
to develop that would bring necessary contextualization to the
definition of papal infallibility. The minority, perhaps, did not
adequately anticipate the way that their strategy of silence would
allow the majority, who did not recognize the same need for caution, to set the tone for the presentation and interpretation of the
council's formulations. While the minority insisted that Vatican I
was unfinished and that questions remained, the majority sought
to establish precisely the opposite view. The majority denied that

---

[18] "Newman to Alfred Plummer, April 3, 1871," in *The Letters and Diaries of John
Henry Newman*, vol. 24, ed. Charles Dessian, et al. (London: Clarendon Press,
1969), 355.

[19] Ibid., 364.

any unsettled matters remained which the conciliar texts could not themselves satisfy. Because they considered the council complete, they understood its decrees to be immediately and absolutely binding. To that end, they judged that acceptance of these decrees was a condition of enjoying full communion with Rome. Representing this position, the French periodical *Le Francais* noted, "The definition has put an end to all controversy; what has become for every Catholic a matter of dogma, has passed completely out of the domain of public opinion."[20] Ultimately, the minority bishops' use of silence as a strategy for holding open the possibility of bringing Vatican I to a proper conclusion allowed the majority's interpretation to be heard all the more loudly and clearly.

In this context where the maximalist interpretation came to be seen, by many, as the appropriate reading of Vatican I, German chancellor Otto von Bismarck authored a letter which accused the council of declaring the pope sovereign and absolute monarch of the church and consequently reducing the bishops to mere tools (*Werkzeuge*) of the pope. Bismarck argued that the pope now had more power than any absolute monarch in history and that this elevation of his authority would have grave consequences for church-state relations. The German bishops responded to this accusation in the Collective Declaration of 1875 which became a critical document for the interpretation of Vatican I. Their response insists that the bishops' authority is in no way diminished by Vatican I's teaching on papal authority. The declaration says:

> It is in virtue of the same divine institution upon which the papacy rests that the episcopate also exists. It, too, has its rights and duties, because of the ordinance of God himself, and the Pope has neither the right nor the power to change them. Thus it is a complete misunderstanding of the Vatican decrees to believe that because of them "episcopal jurisdiction has been absorbed into the papal," that the Pope has "in principle taken the place of each individual bishop," that the bishops are now "no more than tools of the Pope, his officials, without responsibility of their own."[21]

---

[20] Butler, *The Vatican Council*, 2:169.
[21] See *The Christian Faith in the Doctrinal Documents of the Catholic Church*, ed. J. Neuner and J. Dupuis, 6th ed. (New York: Alba House, 1996), 841.

The declaration gained prominence when Pope Pius IX took the step of formally showing his approval of the text in a consistorial allocution on March 15, 1875. With this endorsement, Pius rejected the maximalizing ultramontane interpretation of Vatican I. The pope's endorsement also suggests that the full meaning of the council's teachings are not completely clear within the texts themselves. Thus, the German bishops' declaration and the pope's support of it convey that, despite the maximalists' efforts, open questions remained regarding Vatican I's interpretation.

While questions persisted regarding the right reading of *Pastor Aeternus*, as time moved on conversations on this topic began to shift. As the debates of the council grew more distant, it seemed to many in the minority that the faithful had, in fact, accepted Vatican I's teachings so that further debates on these matters would only have deleterious outcomes. Many of the minority bishops also came to realize that the problems which they anticipated with the definition did not, in fact, materialize. For instance, fears that the promulgation of *Pastor Aeternus* would result in mass conversions to Protestant denominations or catalyze a major schism did not come to pass. Bishop Foulon of Nancy (France) wrote that despite his fears about the divisive potential of a definition of papal infallibility, "the church in fact remains very united."[22] Further, the escalation of military conflict and social instability related to the Franco-Prussian War deflected attention away from the seemingly abstract matters of the council to other kinds of clear and present dangers.[23] Continuing to call attention to the problems inherent in the conciliar texts seemed only to

[22] See O'Gara, *Triumph in Defeat*, 202. Rejecting *Pastor Aeternus*, some Catholics in Austria, Germany, and Switzerland did eventually leave the Roman Catholic Church and formed the Old Catholic Churches. Among these Catholics was Döllinger, who was excommunicated from the Roman Catholic Church in 1871.

[23] Archbishop Kenrick of St. Louis remarks that "the outburst of war" had served to "distract the minds of men from reflecting upon the monstrous act that had just been performed, and so to delay a little, and perhaps to mitigate, the inevitable revulsion of thoughtful minds in the Roman-catholic church from the 'sacrifice of the intellect' which was now demanded of them in the much-abused name of the Christian faith." See Kenrick, *An Inside View of the Vatican Council*, 216.

prolong the hostility that had erupted at the council while potentially dividing the faithful.

While explicit debate on the status of Vatican I and its formulations was eventually abandoned, the force of its unanswered questions did not subside. The reception of the decree demanded that Christians think widely about its impact in several areas of life and thought. In that sense, the urgency and import of the matters left undecided by the council were so pressing that they could not be ignored or eradicated by the majority's insistence that they were unimportant or nonexistent. On the contrary, awareness of Vatican I's limited depiction of papal authority became more pronounced over time as the church struggled to navigate the day-to-day aspects of its ecclesiastical, political, and pastoral interests. Thus, rather than receding into the distance, questions regarding the church's infallibility, the origin and nature of the bishops' power, and the relation between episcopal and papal authority accelerated and sought resolution.

While questions regarding episcopal power persisted and grew, they gradually became detached from concerns over the validity of Vatican I itself. This is a critical historical development. The broader debates on the church's nature and authority which had been expected to take place when Vatican I resumed were not left in abeyance when the council's prorogation extended for years; instead, these questions continued outside of the conciliar forum. Beyond the walls of St. Peter's, however, these questions could not be so easily shaped and controlled. Thus, attention shifted to what was not settled—the nature of the bishops' power. Separating the question of episcopal authority from other concerns regarding the council itself allowed this issue to emerge as a legitimate topic in its own right. This shift was important in that it allowed the attention of the whole church, not just those critical of Vatican I, to focus on these issues.

The result of letting go of questions regarding the validity of Vatican II was that issues regarding the nature and mission of the church and, particularly, matters regarding the local churches and local authority surfaced as dominant themes in theological discussions in the decades following Vatican I. In the hundred years after Vatican I, theological conversations became so focused on ecclesiological questions that this period has often been called "the century of the church."[24] Thus, somewhat ironically, an unintended consequence of Vatican I is that it transformed the church's failure to treat the topic of local authority from a nonissue into what might be called a deafening silence. *Pastor Aeternus* provided a leaven which catalyzed deeper and wider consideration of authority and the very nature of the church. In the decades following Vatican I, Newman's observations about incomplete conciliar definitions would be proven correct, and the council's silences would prove impossible to ignore. In that sense, Vatican I, in its positive teaching, its silences, and its limitation, set a framework for the way that the conversations which came after it would unfold.

---

[24] Michael Himes discusses this idea in his article, "The Development of Ecclesiology: Modernity to the Twentieth Century," in *The Gift of the Church: A Textbook on Ecclesiology in Honor of Patrick Granfield, OSB*, ed. Peter Phan (Collegeville, MN: Liturgical Press, 2000), 63.

CHAPTER FIVE

Recognizing Vatican I as a Context for Vatican II

Outstanding questions are not disposed of by being simply ignored;
the result is merely that they pop up again with renewed vigor when
everything seems to have been settled.[1]

—Hans Küng

On January 25, 1959, the newly elected Pope John XXIII made a stunning announcement. He declared his intention to convene an ecumenical council. He disclosed his plans to a group of unsuspecting cardinals who had assembled at the Basilica of St. Paul's Outside the Walls for the conclusion of the Octave of Prayer for Christian Unity. The pope's announcement began by stating that the council's purpose lay in promoting "the good of souls and of the very clear and definite correspondence of the new pontificate to the spiritual needs of the present hour."[2] He spoke of the importance of reaffirming doctrine and discipline and how such efforts at renewal had strengthened the church throughout many critical moments in her history. He then indicated two aims for the council. The first was to promote the "enlightenment, edification and joy of the entire Christian people," and the second was

---

[1] Küng, *Infallible?*, 65.

[2] John XXIII, "Pope John's Announcement of Ecumenical Council," in *Council Daybook Vatican II*, Sessions 1 and 2, ed. Floyd Anderson (Washington, DC: National Catholic Welfare Conference, 1965), 1.

to extend "a renewed cordial invitation to the faithful of the separated communities to participate with us in this quest for unity and grace, for which so many souls long in all parts of the world."[3] Later, the pope recorded that the cardinals had received his announcement in "impressive, devout silence."[4]

News of the pope's decision traveled quickly across the globe. The prospect of a council, while shocking on many levels, was generally met with excitement and enthusiasm. As word of the council spread, one of the first questions which formed in the minds of many observers was whether the gathering proposed by John XXIII would, in fact, be a resumption of the council prorogued in 1870. In other words, would this be a "new" council or an effort to complete the "old" one? This issue sparked intense interest and uncertainty. A few weeks after the announcement, the Canadian Bishops' Conference published a document which gave voice to the question that many were asking: "Would or would not the Council be a continuation of the Council of Pius IX?"[5] While John XXIII's announcement, therefore, triggered many reactions and set multiple activities in motion, one immediate effect was that it highlighted the force of Vatican I's unanswered questions and the way that both its explicit teachings and its silences exerted a determining effect on the church's conversations. Therefore, when John XXIII called for a council to deal with the needs of the "present hour," many immediately expected that this would involve addressing the limitations of Vatican I. In this way, from its earliest days, thoughts about the gathering proposed by John XXIII were linked to matters left unresolved in 1870.

I. The Idea for a Council Emerges

The idea to hold a council arose early in John XXIII's pontificate. The first formal mention of such a possibility occurred in a conversation between the pope and the Vatican Secretary of State,

---

[3] Ibid.

[4] Giuseppe Alberigo, "The Announcement of the Council from the Security of the Fortress to the Lure of the Quest," in Alberigo and Komonchak, *History of Vatican II*, 1:1–54, at 2.

[5] Ibid., 22.

Cardinal Domenico Tardini, regarding the crises facing the modern world and how the church could help alleviate men's and women's suffering.[6] While discussing with Tardini how the church might serve as an instrument of peace amid the challenges of the day, Pope John had the idea, which he later described as "a flash of heavenly light," to convene an ecumenical council.[7] Regarding the origin of this initiative Pope John wrote:

> A question was raised in a meeting I had with the Secretary of State, Cardinal Tardini, which led on to a discussion about the way that the world was plunged into so many grave anxieties and troubles. One thing we noted was that though everyone said they wanted peace and harmony unfortunately conflicts grew more acute and threats multiplied. What should the Church do? Should Christ's mystical barque simply drift along, tossed this way and that by the ebb and flow of the tides? Instead of issuing new warnings, shouldn't she stand out as a beacon of light?[8]

The pope's words illumine important elements about *why* he decided to call a council. They indicate that, from its inception, John XXIII conceived of the gathering as a means of reaching out to the world and demonstrating the church's ability to promote peace and human flourishing. His account indicates also that, even in the earliest stages, the council did not intend to issue condemnations but to present the church as a "beacon of light" within the world.

John XXIII's plan of convening an ecumenical council emerged from his sense that the world was not only undergoing dramatic changes but also that it stood at the threshold of a new era. The developments unfolding in the mid-twentieth century were fast and extensive, and their force was intensified by dynamic advances

---

[6] For an account of the pope's decision to call a council see Peter Hebblethwaite, *John XXIII: Pope of the Council* (London: Geoffrey Chapman, 1984).

[7] In subsequent reflections on this decision, Pope John noted that he had not considered holding a council prior to this "unexpected illumination." He commented, "I do not like to appeal to special inspiration. I am satisfied with the orthodox teaching that everything is from God. In light of that teaching I regarded the idea of a Council as likewise an inspiration from heaven." For a more full account see Alberigo, "The Announcement of the Council," 3–8.

[8] Hebblethwaite, *John XXIII: Pope of the Council*, 316.

in communications, transportation, and media.[9] The world was emerging from the traumatic events of two world wars and the Holocaust that had given the twentieth century the distinction of being "the bloodiest of all centuries."[10] Women and men were also experiencing acute anxieties as a result of the Cold War where the threat of nuclear annihilation seemed, at times, to present a real possibility. There was a growing consensus that the world as a whole had moved beyond monolithic solutions and past unquestioned acceptance of traditional ways of thinking and acting. This fostered the conviction that institutional structures needed to be more flexible in order to meet the needs and expectations of contemporary men and women.[11] Amid these fast and decisive developments, a certain sense of ambiguity and anxiety persisted about the future; that is, while the world was changing quickly, it seemed as if it "was still unsure of which direction to take."[12]

As a historian, John XXIII understood the way in which councils often concurred with the great turning points of history. Within the rapid changes and approach of a new millennium, he saw a crucial opportunity for the church to "define clearly and distinguish between what is sacred principle and eternal gospel and what belongs rather to the changing times."[13] It was clear to him that the church needed to act quickly if it wanted to assist the world in deciding "which direction to take" rather than being regarded as the relic of a previous age. Given his sense of history, the pope considered gathering the universal church in its most authoritative and solemn setting to be a fitting way of meeting this monumental moment on the world stage. John XXIII under-

[9] A masterful account of this period is found in Étienne Fouilloux's chapter, "The Antepreparatory Phase: The Slow Emergence from Inertia (January, 1959–October, 1962)," in Alberigo and Komonchak, *History of Vatican II*, 1:55–166.

[10] Schloesser, "Against Forgetting: Memory, History, Vatican II," 95.

[11] For a study of the factors propelling the modern world into a new era see: Giacomo Martina, "The Historical Context in Which the Idea of a New Ecumenical Council Was Born." *In Vatican II: Assessment and Perspectives Twenty-Five Years After (1962–1987)*, ed. René Latourelle (New York: Paulist Press, 1988) i, 3–73.

[12] Fouilloux, "The Antepreparatory Phase," 56.

[13] Alberigo, "The Announcement of the Council," 3–4.

stood and admired the way that previous councils had been able to foster ages of renewal in the church that had "yielded especially effective results for the strengthening of religious unity and the kindling of a more intense Christian fervor."[14] Unlike many previous councils, however, that had reacted to historic trends or doctrinal controversies by seeking to distance the church from the world, the council the pope envisioned would seek to bring the church up-to-date and offer its services in dealing with contemporary problems.

John XXIII was certain that the church was capable of playing a more dynamic role in finding solutions to the crises facing the world. His sense was that the challenges confronting the world were not necessarily new but demanded new solutions.[15] It was clear to him that the church's role in these conversations had diminished not because it lacked resources for engaging these issues but due to a perception that the Christian message was incoherent or incompatible with modern sensibilities. As such, he discerned that the path forward lay in determining more appropriate ways for the Christian community to express its timeless message as intelligible and relevant. Whereas in the past the church had tried to assert itself doctrinally, the pope envisioned a church that would assert itself pastorally, working from the stores of its wisdom. The council would not focus on the formulation of new doctrine but on the application of existing doctrine to particular contemporary problems.[16]

While John XXIII's idea for a council was bold, especially given the infancy of his papacy, it was not without precedent in the twentieth century. The possibility of calling a council had already been explored by Pius XI and Pius XII, both of whom had initiated steps in this direction. Interestingly, in each instance, the possibility of gathering the universal church was conceived in terms of

[14] Alberigo, "The Announcement of the Council," 2.

[15] John XXIII's choice of a pastoral orientation for the council represented, as Karl Rahner put it, an overcoming of the maximalists' sense after Vatican I that "everything important in theology has already been solved," rendering that position an "old-fashioned theology."

[16] For more on John XXIII's idea of a pastoral council see Alberigo, "The Announcement of the Council," especially 33–54.

resuming and completing the unfinished work of Vatican I. In 1923, Pius XI briefly considered assembling the universal church as a means of promoting Catholic unity after the divisive and destructive effects of the First World War. He soon abandoned this idea, however, as too laborious an undertaking.[17] While the efforts of Pius XI were not very developed, those of Pius XII were quite extensive. Pius XII gave sustained thought and energy to the possibility of convening a council for the purpose of demonstrating Catholic unity, condemning protracted modern errors, and formally defining, by acclamation, the teaching on Mary's assumption. He anticipated that the gathering would be short and would provide a sign of Catholic strength and unity while requiring only a few weeks of preparatory time and deliberation.[18] In 1948, Pius XII went so far as to send out a letter requesting that the bishops submit their thoughts on the advisability of such an endeavor. Sixty-five bishops responded positively and expressed genuine enthusiasm for his proposal. Notably, John XXIII, then papal nuncio in Paris, was one of those who replied favorably to the idea.[19]

Even as Pius XII's suggestion received a good deal of support, it also engendered considerable debate. Enthusiasm for a council was drowned out by controversy over the appropriate topics for discussion, the suitability of the historical context, and matters of organizational etiquette. The tensions brewing in Europe following the Second World War also siphoned attention and energy away from efforts to develop a council. Eventually, Pius XII became so discouraged by the debates sparked by his proposal and the complexity of its execution that he abandoned it altogether. He reasoned that he could achieve the same ends, with less rancor, if he adjudicated these matters himself. Subsequently, he attended to the subjects he viewed most pressing by defining the doctrine of Mary's assumption in 1950 and issuing the encyclical *Humani*

[17] For an account of Pius XI's brief consideration of a council, see Robin Anderson, *Between Two Wars: The Story of Pope Pius XI* (Chicago: Franciscan Herald Press, 1977).

[18] It is interesting to note that Cardinal Alfredo Ottaviani, who would play a large role at Vatican II, was one of the main proponents of this initiative.

[19] See: S. Oddi, *"Aux origins du Concile: la défaite du 'parti romain,'" Catholica* 42, no. 8 (1988): 34–49.

Generis as a condemnation of the lingering errors of Modernism. Pius sought decisive action on these issues and originally presumed that a council would support and lend force to his efforts. When the realities of a council promised to complicate and, perhaps, even undermine his plans, he opted to resolve these matters using the tools of papal authority. This served as evidence, for some, that the fast and efficient exercise of the pope's teaching authority made the use of councils obsolete. *(Conversation)*

John XXIII was largely unaware of the details of his predecessors' efforts as he developed his own thoughts about a council. There is no evidence to suggest that he considered the upcoming council as a resumption of Vatican I. His own sense was that the bishops were hungry for a gathering and that it would be well received if oriented toward the right issues. He was not naïve, however, about the massive difficulty of such an undertaking and the risk that a council pursued for the sake of unity could, in fact, be the cause of great division. The cumulative effects of these insights enhanced the pope's sense that the council should allow for as much deliberation among the bishops as possible and should avoid approaching modern issues with a predominantly defensive stance. He discerned that greater internal unity and effective external communication could be achieved by focusing on the goals shared by the church and modern society and by highlighting the positive contribution that the Gospel could make toward these ends. The pope was confident that while a council would be welcomed by the bishops, a continuation of the church's consuming battle against modern errors could not dominate its agenda.

John XXIII convoked the council on December 25, 1961, with the apostolic constitution *Humanae Salutis*. While this event elicited further excitement, details of the gathering remained notably vague. The absence of specifics regarding the council's agenda left considerable room for a wide range of observers to suggest what the council could or should be about. Important figures produced commentaries and articles on the council's announcement and speculated on a variety of possible matters that it might address.[20] While the suggestions proffered were quite diverse, it is notable

NOT NEW DOCTRINES/NEW UNDERSTANDING OF EXISTING DOCTRINES

[20] See Alberigo, "The Announcement of the Council," 33–44.

that they often predicted or encouraged that the gathering should take up the issues left unresolved by Vatican I. One of the commentaries considered the most authoritative was that of Yves Congar, OP.[21] Congar's text, unsurprisingly, began with a learned discussion of the tradition of ecumenical and general councils. He then outlined five thematic areas for the council's focus. Among these, he recommended that "the teaching on the Church, left incomplete by the discontinuation of the Council of Pius XI, would be completed."[22] Congar's diary from the early phases of the council's development also contains many references concerning the council's need to treat the ecclesiological issues left open by Vatican I, especially the critical issue of the bishops.[23] He expressed confidence that the upcoming gathering would be a new council and not a continuation of Vatican I. The fact that Congar felt the need to express that the upcoming council would be distinct from its predecessor underscores the way that John XXIII's announcement prompted questions about this possibility.

Another influential commentary, written by Otto Karrer, a Swiss priest active in the ecumenical movement, expressed a desire similar to Congar's. He suggested that the council should "abstain from proclaiming any new dogmatic propositions of any kind and [should] reinterpret the definitions of 1870, using for this purpose the declaration of the German bishops in 1875, which Pius IX had approved."[24] In order to facilitate ecumenical relations, Karrer felt that it was important for a council to deal with the issue of episcopal authority while developing a more comprehensive view of the church's nature. Congar's and Karrer's commentaries reflect what Giuseppe Alberigo regards as a general and accepted sense among church leaders and theologians prior to Vatican II. He observes that following the council's announcement, "It was a common view that one of the chief doctrinal aims of the Second Vatican Council would be to complete the ecclesiology of Vatican I

---

[21] "Les conciles dans la vie de l'Église," *Informations catholiques internationals*, no. 90 (February 15, 1959): 17–26.

[22] Alberigo, "The Announcement of the Council," 35.

[23] See Yves Congar, *My Journal of the Council* (Collegeville, MN: Liturgical Press, 2012), 93–95.

[24] Alberigo, "The Announcement of the Council," 23.

by a treatment of the nature of the role of the episcopate in the Church."[25] It was largely taken for granted that one of the council's chief tasks would be to treat questions regarding the nature and mission of the church. This task grew out of the bishops' desire for "an organic and complete dogmatic Constitution on the Church in order to complete Vatican I."[26] Therefore, prior to receiving much information regarding the council's agenda, many assumed that much of the upcoming council's work would arise from issues that had been lingering since 1870.

II. The Bishops' *Vota*

On June 18, 1959, Cardinal Tardini, acting as the president of the council's Antepreparatory Commission, issued a letter inviting the bishops to tender suggestions for the conciliar agenda. His letter requested that the bishops "kindly communicate to this pontifical commission the critiques, suggestions, and wishes which your pastoral concern and your zeal for souls urges you to offer in connection with matters and subjects of possible discussion at the upcoming council, and to do so with complete freedom and honesty."[27] This request concluded with Tardini asking that replies be submitted, in Latin, no later than September 1, 1959. The nature of Tardini's appeal, in itself, reflects the more open and deliberative character that Pope John envisioned for the council. Initially, when the matter of consulting the bishops arose, Tardini proposed distributing a limited questionnaire so that his commission might more easily manage and compile the voluminous responses expected. John XXIII opposed this suggestion in favor of sending a more open-ended request for information in order to elicit from the bishops their real thoughts free from any constrictions. Thus, Tardini's letter inviting the bishops to submit their "opinions," "views," and "suggestions" on "anything which Your

---

[25] Joseph Komonchak, "The Struggle for the Council during the Preparation of Vatican II (1960–1962)," in Alberigo and Komonchak, *History of Vatican II*, 1:167–356, at 293.

[26] Ibid., 285n436.

[27] Fouilloux, "The Antepreparatory Phase," 94.

Excellency thinks it good to discuss and clarify" represented an early victory for Pope John's vision of the council as deliberative and dialogical.[28]

As the months progressed, the bishops' *vota* poured into Rome. Not surprisingly, these *vota* were quite diverse.[29] Such multiplicity might be expected from a collection of 2,000 responses from men throughout the world who had little, if any, contact with one another. In general, the bishops' replies expressed a positive reaction to John XXIII's idea of convening a council. The vast majority of bishops were hopeful that the pope's initiative would reap substantial benefits, and they suggested a wide range of concerns for the council to address. There were, however, a minority of bishops who opposed gathering the universal church on grounds which included concerns that it was "premature" given the theological climate, the belief that the contemporary context was too chaotic to foster authentic conciliar deliberations, and concern that the pontiff's advanced age was prohibitive of such an undertaking.[30]

While a tremendous variety exists in the bishops' submissions, it is still possible and valuable to classify them into two basic categories as Argentinean theologian Fortunato Mallimaci has done.[31]

---

[28] Ibid.

[29] There has been much discussion among scholars regarding the proper use and significance of the *vota* in constructing a view of dispositions among the council fathers and the climate in certain national churches. Questions have been raised regarding exactly how free and representative the responses are. For more comprehensive treatments of these debates see Fouilloux, "The Antepreparatory Phase," 55–166. Also excellent in terms of more concentrated regional studies are Joseph Komonchak, "U.S. Bishops' Suggestions," *Cristianesimo Nella Storia* 15 (1994): 313–71, and *Cristianismo e iglesias de América Latina en vísperas del Vaticano II*, ed. Oscar Beozzo (San Jose, Costa Rica: CEHILA, 1992).

[30] It is interesting to note that the latter two concerns—the chaos of the day and the age of the pope—were also raised when Pope Pius IX announced his plans for the First Vatican Council.

[31] This distinction is developed in Fortunato Mallimaci's piece "Argentina," which analyzes the *vota* from the bishops of this nation. He writes, "*Una primaera lectura muestra la gran diferencia entre aquellos que proponen—y son la mayoría— cambios en el derecho canónico de tal o cual aspecto disciplinario, doctrinario o de funcionamiento cotidiano de la Iglesia, y aquellos interesados en una perspective pastoral, teológica o de cambios profundos,*" in Beozzo, *Cristianismo e Iglesias de América Latina en Vísperas del Vaticano II*. While it is certainly dangerous to overgeneralize the

Mallamaci divides these responses into "canonical" and "pastoral" streams. The majority of the bishops' *vota* fall into the canonical stream, which is characterized by a submissive posture to Rome, juridical vocabulary, a discursive style, and a focus on matters of discipline. In large part, such responses concentrate on modern errors and the need for a defensive posture. Faced with what they perceived to be the same problems of a century ago, only intensified, the *vota* of these bishops are generally devoted to identifying errors and suggesting appropriate condemnations. For example, Bishop Joseph Maxmillian Mueller of Sioux City, Iowa, wrote, "The errors condemned by Pius IX in 1862 have grown worse over the years. Yesterday's rationalism and modernism have degenerated into secularism, materialism and atheistic communism and are powerful not only as theoretical systems but as norms for daily life."[32] Mueller added that these corruptions had taken hold so extensively that they should no longer be attributed to individuals but as having assumed a social character.

The tendency of these responses toward a defensive stance is also represented in the reply of Bishop Bartholome of St. Cloud, Minnesota, who asserted that the need to combat errors should serve as the chief purpose of the council; he wrote, "It is the universal opinion of the priests of our diocese and of the bishop that the calling of the forthcoming Ecumenical Council by Pope John XXIII is appropriate and necessary to correct and to wrest out the errors and false opinions which oppose the faith of the Christian peoples and of Catholics, especially during the last half-century, through the pernicious movements and false doctrines of liberalism and materialism."[33] The *vota* of bishops in the canonical stream advocate a defensive theology which emphasizes the differences between the truth inherent in the church and the corruption of the secular world. These bishops, in many ways,

---

content of the bishops' responses, such a categorization of the bishops' *vota* is in this case helpful and warranted. Caution must be exercised in order to use this tool to the extent that it is helpful but not to exaggerate its usefulness in a way that distorts or reduces the bishops' contributions.

[32] Komonchak, "U.S. Bishops' Suggestions for Vatican II," 328.

[33] Ibid.

echoed sentiments of their predecessors preparing for Vatican I in believing that relativism could only be overcome by securing its opposite—universal truth and reliable access to it.

The *vota* of the "pastoral" stream are characterized by an emphasis on reform and a more theological and pastoral orientation. In general, these letters favor an adaptation of the Catholic Church to its times and often propose concrete solutions to problems they observe in the world and in their particular dioceses. These replies are generally longer and more developed than their canonical counterparts, largely because they include efforts to ground their positions theologically and consider how they might be implemented or applied. The collective response submitted by the bishops of Indonesia is representative of these pastoral *vota*. This group emphasized the need to focus on the universality of the church and argued for "adaptation of Church law and worship to the variety of situations in which the Churches have found themselves; collaboration between local churches; and the participation of the entire Catholic world in its central government."[34] It called for the council to develop a separate chapter on the constitution of the church with an emphasis on the church as the Mystical Body of Christ. This *votum* also recommended the establishment of a curial office that would dialogue with the World Council of Churches and a constitution on the laity.

These pastoral *vota* often include freer and more expansive critiques of the church. Many complained about the complexity and difficulty of navigating Roman bureaucracy and indicated a desire for less institutional centralization. Such responses were not afraid to voice their frustrations with the problems they viewed in the church's own structure. Bishop Helder Câmara, secretary of the Brazilian episcopal conference and vice president of CELAM, reflected the boldness of some in the pastoral stream when he suggested that "Latin not be the language of the Council and that the Church commit itself there to the formation of a better world first of all in economic and social areas, but also in aesthetic, scientific and political areas."[35] While it would be an exaggeration

---

[34] Fouilloux, "The Antepreparatory Phase," 122.
[35] Ibid., 126.

to contend that these responses manifest a deep understanding of the type of *aggiornamento* that would develop at Vatican II, the pastoral *vota* do reflect, in varying degrees, a foreshadowing of the direction that the council would ultimately take. They recognize a need for reform within the church both pastorally and theologically and reflect an appreciation for the connection between the two. These insights would become central to the council's work.

The general multiplicity of viewpoints within the *vota* renders their areas of commonality all the more striking. Despite significant differences in tone, emphases, creativity, and style, a majority of replies in both the pastoral and canonical streams are united by a consensus on three tasks for the council: (1) better definition of the role of the bishop, (2) accelerating liturgical reform, and (3) restoration of the permanent diaconate.[36] Of these three areas of agreement, the first is clearly the most dominant in their responses.[37] The consensus on the need to examine matters of episcopal authority is made clear in the "Final Synthesis of the Resolutions and Suggestions for the Coming Ecumenical Council from Their Excellencies the Bishops and Prelates of the Entire World," dated March 12, 1960. This text reports that a single theme dominates the bishops' suggestions: "the full re-establishment of the authority and power of the bishops in the government of dioceses."[38]

The need to clarify issues related to the nature of the church and, specifically, the exercise of episcopal power, transects both

[36] Ibid., 109.

[37] The high level of agreement on the need to clarify the role of the bishop is illustrated by the response of Bishop Thomas McCabe of Wollongong, Australia. Three months past the September deadline, McCabe sent a brief letter to the Antepreparatory Commission indicating that he had no original ideas to contribute regarding the conciliar agenda. Apologizing for the delay in his response, he offers that he could think of nothing important to suggest "except that some thought be given to the power and authority of the bishops." McCabe's admission that he is unable to devise any unique suggestions for the council's deliberations and can think of nothing other than the obvious necessity of discussing the nature of episcopal power highlights the fact that the need to treat the matter of episcopal power was largely taken for granted. See Fouilloux, "The Antepreparatory Phase," 99.

[38] Ibid., 148.

streams of *vota*.[39] The bishops in the canonical stream attempt to alleviate the imbalance between episcopal and papal authority by extending Vatican I's description of the pope's authority to the office of the local ordinary. In other words, they seek to balance the limited effects of Vatican I's focus on centralized papal authority by instilling that same type of power in the bishop. Their hope was that the upcoming council's decrees "would turn each bishop into a pope in his own diocese."[40] Therefore, while the canonical stream recognizes the problems related to Vatican I's lack of clarity regarding episcopal authority, it does not identify the underlying theology which led to this situation as problematic. Rather, they seek to fill the silence left by Vatican I by extending a maximalist theology. The *vota* of the pastoral stream argue for the practical and theological warrants of instilling more pastoral discretion in the hands of the local ordinary. They suggest that the flaws inherent in Vatican I's portrayal of papal power should be remedied by depicting ecclesiastical authority through the lens of the church's history and mission. The *votum* of the faculty of The Catholic University of America captures the sense of many in the pastoral camp by asserting that the council should engage in "a vindication of the authority of the bishops."[41] Several even go so far as to provide a theological foundation for such a reevaluation. A common theme for this foundation is the sacramental nature of the episcopal office. In his *votum*, Bishop Vagnozzi, an Italian serving as apostolic delegate to the United States, expressed his hope for a conciliar definition which affirms that "episcopal consecration is truly a sacrament by which a character is imprinted for the performing of acts which are proper and exclusive to bishops."[42] Vagnozzi's hope represents a theme consistent throughout the pastoral *vota*, namely, a desire to clarify and contextualize the power of the bishops by developing a picture of ecclesial authority more in line with the rest of Christian tradition.

The massive amount of correspondence which flooded the Pontifical Antepreparatory Commission of the council represented a

---

[39] Ibid., 99.
[40] Ibid., 109.
[41] Komonchak, "U.S. Bishops' Suggestions for Vatican II," 369.
[42] Ibid., 335.

"panorama of opinions and suggestions."[43] It became clear that, amid the diversity of the bishops' experiences and expectations, they shared a sense that the council had to address ecclesiological issues and specifically the rights and responsibilities of the episcopate. This agreement reveals that, regardless of their theological sensibilities, the experience of the unbalanced presentation of the church following Vatican I oriented the bishops' gaze to larger issues related to the church and to the exercise of local authority, in particular. The suggestions contained in the *vota* do not represent a desire to supersede or overcome the teachings of Vatican I. On the contrary, both the pastoral and canonical streams often reflect a desire both explicitly and implicitly to build on Vatican I's teachings by treating its silences.[44] Interestingly, they seek to do this in converse ways. The *vota* of both the pastoral and the canonical streams indicate that, regardless of being divided on many theological matters, the absence of a clear treatment of episcopal authority was, perhaps, the most pressing issue facing the church. Moreover, until this lacuna was addressed, it hindered the future council's ability to deal effectively with other issues. The desire to focus on the bishops, amidst all the diversity of the concerns expressed in the *vota*, reflects in a powerful way the lingering force of Vatican I's unanswered questions.

Shortly after the request for *vota* was sent out, but before the massive work of compiling the council's preparatory documents began, John XXIII communicated to Cardinal Tardini that the upcoming gathering would be named the Second Vatican Council. Pope John was not explicit about his reasons for this choice. In a journal entry dated July 4, 1959, he recorded, "When I got back to

---

[43] Luciano Casimirri, "Suggestions from the World's Bishops on Council Agenda Classified," in Anderson, *Council Daybook Vatican II*, Sessions 1 and 2, p. 3.

[44] Significantly, what does not generally appear in the *vota* of either stream is much discussion of the question of papal infallibility. This "silence" reflects the fact that the bishops' accepted that this topic had been definitively treated and was no longer a matter of debate. Papal infallibility would be affirmed at Vatican II and its texts would ultimately cite *Pastor Aeternus* numerous times. Yet, at this earlier stage of choosing a direction for the council, there was not a great amount of interest in talking about papal infallibility, given that this matter was settled and many believed it had consumed too much attention already.

the house, I found that the ecumenical council now in preparation ought to be called 'the Second Vatican Council' because the last one, celebrated by Pope Pius IX in 1870, bore the name of Vatican Council I—Vatican *le premier*."[45] The decision that the new council would be named Vatican II meant that it was free to follow its own agenda without being forced to bring to a conclusion all of the issues left unresolved by Vatican I. Commenting on this decision, Alberigo notes that "it was necessary, in fact, to get rid of the uncertainties that were abroad about the possible reopening of the Council that had been suspended in 1870."[46] In addition to revealing that the upcoming gathering would be a new council and not a resumption of the council prorogued in 1870, the selection of the name Vatican II also suggested its location. The council would be held in Rome at St. Peter's Basilica, in the same place where the bishops had deliberated in 1869 and 1870. The decision that the council would be named Vatican II clearly demarcated a separation between Pius IX's council and John XXIII's, yet at the same time, this choice also indicated a significant continuity between them.

III. Developing an Overall Plan for the Council

The process of reading, organizing, and considering the *vota* in order to devise the council's preparatory documents or schemata took place between June 1960 and February 1962.[47] Despite the enormous amount of work devoted to this effort, the bishops

[45] Alberigo, "The Announcement of the Council," 50.

[46] Ibid. Regardless of the desire to give the council a name in order, in part, to end speculation that the event was a continuation of Vatican I, Thomas Holland notes that some "fastened on to the title of 'Vatican II' and saw the main objective as the completion of the unfinished business left over from Vatican I. In part, they were thinking of what was often traded as Vatican I's image of the church: a single peak soaring aloft from a flat plain. They saw Vatican II going exclusively, or at least in a very big way, for bishops." See Thomas Holland, "The Church Comes of Age," in *Vatican II Revisited by Those Who Were There*, 49–60, at 50.

[47] This arduous and complex task is well documented by Komonchak in his chapter "The Struggle for the Council during the Preparation of Vatican II (1960–1962)," 167–356.

generally greeted these texts with dissatisfaction. The bishops' disappointment was not directed at any one particular formulation in these documents, but, as Joseph Ratzinger noted, the reaction was directed at the "spirit behind the preparatory work."[48] Rather than reflecting the vision articulated by John XXIII, the schemata seemed to provide a defense of the neoscholastic Christian philosophy, which many bishops hoped the council would move beyond. While John had ignited hopes that the council would open the church to engaging the world in new ways, the proposed schemata seemed to suggest that nothing had changed from the days of Pius XII. Representing the views of many, Congar criticized the schemata for their "neglect of the substantive content of the Gospel, negative view of the contemporary world, abstract and scholastic style, and omission of crucial current issues and lack of ecumenical interest."[49] Additional concerns regarding these texts stemmed from their excessive number and failure to provide a cohesive vision for the bishops' work. These anxieties were intensified by the fact that the eyes of the world were on the church, waiting to see if this ancient institution would actually engage in the updating it had announced. Many worried that the schemata which had been developed would not allow for the type of deliberation or renewal that John XXIII had signaled and that they would, in fact, only further entrench the church in its defensive posture and negative assessment of the world. This would mean that in a very public way the church would appear unwilling or incapable of updating itself, just as its critics expected.

Alarmed about the state of the preparatory texts and the failure to "formulate a radical strategy, a single main plan," Cardinal Leon Josef Suenens, archbishop of Malines and primate of Belgium, spoke with Pope John about these issues during an audience in March 1962.[50] Suenens expressed concerns that the documents were too numerous, inconsistent in quality, and focused on particulars rather than basic principles. He urged that the number of

---

[48] Leon Josef Suenens, "A Plan for the Whole Council," in *Vatican II Revisited by Those Who Were There* (Minneapolis, MN: Winston Press, 1986), 88–105, at 88.

[49] Komonchak, "The Struggle for the Council during the Preparation of Vatican II (1960–1962)," 234.

[50] Suenens, "A Plan for the Whole Council," 88.

schema be reduced and that the remaining texts be arranged in an order that would reflect a coherent direction for the gathering.[51] Upon hearing Suenens's thoughts, John XXIII responded by asking the cardinal to devise a plan for the council that would outline a clear direction for its work while making maximal use of the existing schemata which had been the product of considerable effort. In his account of this meeting Suenens writes:

> During an audience with the Pope in March 1962, I complained to John XXIII about the number of schemata prepared for discussion at the forthcoming Council, which seemed quite excessive. There were, I believe seventy-two of them, very uneven in value, and in any case so overwhelming in volume that *a priori* they prevented fruitful and worthwhile work at the Council itself. John XXIII asked me to clear the ground and submit to him a plan based on the prepared schemata.[52]

Approximately a month after this conversation, Suenens sent John XXIII a preliminary sketch of his proposal. He notes that this initial plan was "designed to cut out a lot of dead wood and set the Council on a truly pastoral course."[53] Pleased with Suenens's work, Pope John offered two suggestions. The first was that Suenens elicit the opinions of some influential cardinals who might help him develop his thoughts even further. Among those the pope recommended were Cardinals Giovanni Battista Montini (Milan), Achille Liénart (Lille), Giuseppe Siri (Genoa), and Julius Döpfner (Münich). Second, John XXIII encouraged Suenens to read Fr. Léon Dehon's *Il diario del Concilio Vaticano I* as a part of his preparations. Suenens accepted both ideas enthusiastically.

In a letter dated July 4, 1962, Suenens reported back to John XXIII on his meeting with the cardinals that he had recommended. Suenens noted that the session which had taken place at the Belgian College was "relaxed" and "friendly" and that those present were in agreement on many issues.[54] He conveyed that those gath-

---

[51] Ibid., 89.
[52] Ibid.
[53] Ibid.
[54] Ibid., 90.

ered concurred that the council should begin with a constitution on the church "in the hope that the Second Vatican Council might really be the Council *De Ecclesia*."[55] With this important point of consensus, Suenens remarked that the next task would be to "work out a more detailed plan showing where and how the finished schemata would find a place in the overall framework as set out."[56] At the conclusion of his letter, Suenens included his impressions of Dehon's diary of Vatican I. Of this volume, Suenens writes, "It is full of interest and life and at the same time indications of what should be done . . . and what should not be done."[57]

Suenens submitted a final version of his plan to John XXIII shortly after the meeting at the Belgian College. The text is relatively short—a brief seven pages—and speaks in clear, straightforward, and nontechnical terms. It begins by suggesting that Vatican II should be organized in a way which gives it a "pastoral, coherent overall direction that all can easily grasp."[58] He recommends that it be "put together like a triptych, its three parts being: a basic introduction, the major themes grouped under four main headings, and a final message which would be a sort of apotheosis of the Council."[59] Suenens suggests streamlining the bishops' work by centering all of their deliberations on a single question: "How is the Church of the twentieth century measuring up to the Master's last command: Go, therefore, make disciples of all nations. Baptize them in the name of the Father and of the Son and of the Holy Spirit and teach them to observe the commands I gave you? (cf. Mathew 28:19)."[60] This command, Suenens argues, naturally leads to the basic idea of his plan. This "basic idea" is that the council's deliberations should be organized into two main categories: considering the church in its own internal life (*ad intra*) and considering the church's relation to the world (*ad extra*). Such a

---

[55] Ibid., 95.
[56] Ibid.
[57] Ibid., 96.
[58] Ibid.
[59] Ibid.
[60] Ibid., 97.

strategy, Suenens argues, would provide order and clarity while allowing for the greatest possible use of the existing schemata.

After a brief introduction, Suenens's text opens with a section titled "Overall approach of the plan."[61] This section starts with the heading "Schema *'De Ecclesiae Christi mysterio'* as a starting point."[62] It begins: "As a start, it seems necessary to link the Second Vatican Council to the First. The best way of doing this would be to begin the Council with discussion of a schema *De Ecclesiae Christi mysterio*."[63] Suenens then goes on to list five reasons indicating why such a starting point is appropriate. The first three are worth quoting in their entirety:

> (a) Continuity with Vatican I. The First Vatican Council had prepared a schema *De Ecclesia*, of which it was able to define only one part: papal primacy and infallibility. It did not have time to "place" the bishops or the laity in the mystery of the Church.

> (b) Better doctrinal balance. This would be both a work of continuity and the achievement of a better balance, since the mystery of the Church would thereby appear in its fullness in complete harmony.

> (c) A step towards our separated brethren. The Orthodox reproach the Church with not giving bishops their due place; the Protestants reproach it for not giving the laity their proper place. In this schema *De Ecclesia Christi Mysterio* we would well reply to their objections in a positive manner by showing the link between the Papacy and the Body of the Church, by demonstrating the place and meaning of the episcopal college and by stressing the role of the laity (all this will be dealt with in more detail later).

From the beginning Suenens is clear that his "overall approach" to the council is rooted in the fact that it is "necessary to link the Second Vatican Council to the First." Also significant is that when he moves on to articulating the rationale for choosing the church as the central theme of the council he, again, begins by citing the importance of continuity with Vatican I. His first reason explicitly refers to the unfinished character of Vatican I, referencing the

---

[61] Suenens, "A Plan for the Whole Council," 97.
[62] Ibid.
[63] Ibid.

original *De Ecclesia* schema. He notes that Vatican I was able to develop "only one part: papal primacy and infallibility" in that it "did not have time to 'place' the bishops or the laity in the mystery of the Church." Suenens, therefore, recommends the church as the primary theme of the upcoming council not only because of the innate importance of this topic but also because of the importance of maintaining continuity with Vatican I.

While Suenens's first rationale is the only one which explicitly refers to Vatican I, when read carefully, it is clear that the first three of his reasons all pertain to Vatican I. Suenens's second argument for selecting the church as the council's focus also has Vatican I at the center. Here, he states the need for the council to achieve "better doctrinal balance" so that the mystery of the church might "appear in its fullness in complete harmony." His mention of the "work of continuity" and the need for "better doctrinal balance" clearly refer to the limited or unbalanced presentations of the church that dominated following Vatican I, a condition which he acknowledged in his first rationale. Suenens's third reason—the need to take "a step towards our separated brethren"—also references issues directly connected to Vatican I. Here, Suenens notes that treating the subject of the church immediately would allow the council to reply to concerns about Vatican I's presentation of the papacy and its connection to the rest of the church raised by Protestants and the Orthodox. This ecumenical dimension accords with John XXIII's original vision of the council. Suenens believed that addressing these concerns at the outset of the council would allow for a better context for dialogue and dealing with other ecumenically sensitive issues.[64]

---

[64] Congar notes in several points in his diary that renewing the church's ecclesiology was essential for advancing the council's ecumenical goals. He observed that, for the most part, the Protestant and Orthodox observers at the council were far more interested in the schema on the church than the schema on ecumenism. They recognized that nothing important and meaningful could be said about ecumenism if there was no movement away from a defensive and juridical model of church. He records one such conversation with some Orthodox observers: "They told me: these texts ON ecumenism are not very important: an anthropology and a pneumatology in the *De Ecclesia* would be the most positive ECUMENICAL step." See Congar, *My Journal of the Council*, 383.

After presenting the theme of the church as the proper starting point for Vatican II, Suenens's proposal moves on to discuss his recommendation that the council be organized around two poles: the church *ad intra* and the church *ad extra*. He considers these poles in two clear sections: "Section A: *Ecclesia 'ad intra'*" and "Section B: *Ecclesia 'ad extra.'*" Within each of these divisions, Suenens correlates a particular aim for the council with an aspect of Christ's command in Matthew 28:20. In Section A, he suggests that concerns related to the church's internal life could be grouped around the first half of Matthew's text:

> Go, therefore: *Ecclesia evangelizans (or salvificans)*
> Make disciples of all nations: *Ecclesia docens*
> Baptize them: *Ecclesia sancticans*
> In the name of the Father . . . : *Ecclesia orans.*[65]

In this section, Suenens devotes the greatest amount of time, by far, to treating the first category, *Ecclesia evangelizans*. He emphasizes the need for "a major declaration on the subject of the apostolic college and the role of the bishops at the heart of the Church."[66] He underscores the importance of clarifying the role proper to the bishop as head of the overall pastoral work of his diocese. Accordingly, he argues for the need to strengthen the powers of the bishops in regards to three major concerns: *in se* (in themselves); *quoad religiosos exemptos individualiter* (in relation to individual exempt religious); and *quoad religiosos exemptos collective prout adunantur in Unionibus Superiorum Maiorum* (in relation to exempt religious collectively, inasmuch as they are incardinated in congregations under major superiors). It is significant that Suenens's plan for the council begins not only with the church but also with the church *ad intra* and, in particular, with the nature of the bishops' authority. He prioritizes the need to gain clarity regarding the power of the bishops and to strengthen their authority so that they might act effectively and, therefore, lead the church in its efforts to "carry the Good News to all creation."[67] Here, we see that

---

[65] Suenens, "A Plan for the Whole Council," 97.

[66] Ibid., 98.

[67] Ibid.

Suenens's division of the church *ad extra* and *ad intra* is not just an organizational tool but speaks to fundamental elements of the church's life and their inherent interconnection.

In his consideration of the church *ad intra*, Suenens does not substantively engage issues related to the papacy. His plan is virtually silent on this topic. In treating the church *ad intra*, Suenens's emphasis is overwhelmingly on clarifying and strengthening the nature of episcopal authority. While Suenens had lamented to Pope John XXIII that plans for the council were hindered by being bogged down in particulars rather than focusing on basic principles, in regard to the issue of episcopal authority, Suenens is clear about the need for the council to address numerous particulars. Suenens's choice to focus on the church in general and the authority of the bishops in particular but not address papal power cannot be understood unless it is seen against the backdrop of Vatican I. It is because Vatican I addressed papal authority in a decisive manner that Suenens's plan does not have to engage this topic. Suenens's silence on the nature of the pope's authority is not a suggestion that he advocates a weak notion of the papacy; it is, instead, a product of his historical and theological context. He considered this issue of papal infallibility settled and was attuned to other questions. Suenens's choice not to engage the topic of papal authority illumines two important points: first, it provides evidence of the way that silence on a particular topic does not always communicate that a reality is unimportant or not valued. Second, it illumines the way that awareness of Vatican I's legacy is critical to properly understanding the development of Vatican II.

After reflecting on how the council might address the church *ad intra*, Suenens shifts to considering topics for the consideration of the church *ad extra*. He notes, "Under this general heading several major problems (detailed later) could be grouped together, falling comfortably into the scope of 'and teach them to observe all of the commands I gave you.'"[68] He advises starting the consideration of the church *ad extra* with a focus on the family. After

---

[68] Ibid., 101.

acknowledging the existence of grave problems and serious anxieties plaguing modern families, he remarks, "What do men look for? Answer: they look for love in the bosom of their families, daily bread for themselves and their families, peace within and between nations. These are the basic aspirations. Can the Church bring them anything on these different levels?"[69] Suenens then lays out, building on existing encyclicals and other ecclesial documents, topics that the council might engage such as birth control, economic realities, religious freedom, and church-state relations. Finally, this section concludes by suggesting that the council conclude with final words that represent a "collective act of faith in Christ living in his Church, according to his promise: 'And know that I am with you always; yes, to the end of time' (Matt 28:20)."[70] Suenens's suggestion of concluding the council in this way highlights the connection between the church's *ad intra* and *ad extra* dimensions. Ending the gathering with an affirmation of Christ's presence in the church was seen as a way of strengthening the faithful for the outreach that the council had identified.

While Suenens's plan was developing, others voiced similar concerns about the excessive number and uneven quality of the schemata as well as the need for a clear direction for the council. Among these was Montini, who would later lead the council as Paul VI. In a letter dated October 18, 1962, Montini echoed Suenens's worry about the state of the council's preparation. Writing to Cardinal Amleto Cicognani, Vatican Secretary of State, Montini begins by lamenting "the lack, or at least the failure to announce the existence of, an organic, thought-out and logical programme for the Council."[71] He notes that the apparent absence of an overall plan "is dangerous for the outcome of the Council; it diminishes its significance; it makes it lose, in the eyes of the world, that vigour of thought and intelligibility on which its efficacy will to a large extent depend. The material that has been prepared does not seem to have a harmonious and unified overall form; it hardly shines out like a beacon over the age and the

---

[69] Ibid.
[70] Ibid., 102.
[71] Ibid., 102–3.

world."[72] Montini's letter generally affirms Suenens's ideas, although it does suggest its own nuances and areas of emphasis for the council.[73] Ultimately, Montini's main concern, like Suenens, is to develop a program for the council's work that will bring direction to its proceedings and help ensure its success.

Montini ventures to provide some "guiding thoughts" for the council.[74] He opts to present his plan in terms of how particular sessions of the gathering would be structured. In all, he proposes that the council's deliberations be divided into three sessions. Like Suenens, Montini begins with the suggestion that the council be focused on the church. Also, like Suenens, he explicitly argues that that this focus is necessary in order to demonstrate continuity with Vatican I. Montini states that:

> The second Vatican Council should be centered around one sole theme: Holy Church [*la santa Chiesa*]. This is required to give continuity with the first Vatican Council, which was interrupted while dealing with this subject. This is what all the bishops want, so as to know exactly what their powers are, following the definition of papal powers, and what the relations are between one and the other. . . . Holy Church: this should be the one and all-embracing theme of this Council; and the vast body of material prepared should be organized around what is obviously its sublime theme.[75]

Montini, like Suenens, roots his plan for the council in the need to engage the questions left unanswered by Vatican I. It is the need to maintain continuity with Vatican I that "requires" a focus on the church and specifically on the local church. Such a focus, according to Montini, is what "all the bishops want" so they can resolve the issue of their own authority and its relation to that of the papacy.

---

[72] Ibid., 103.

[73] Cardinal Luis Antonio Tagle wrote his doctoral dissertation comparing the plans for Vatican II presented by Suenens and Montini. He includes an interesting discussion of the ways that Montini's plans differs in emphasis from Suenens's plan. See Cardinal Luis Antonio Tagle, *Two Plans for the Council: Cardinal Suenens, ecclesia ad intra, ad extra and Cardinal Montini. The Church's Mystery, Mission and Relations* (Networked Digital Library of Theses and Dissertations, 1987), 94–125.

[74] Suenens, "A Plan for the Whole Council," 103.

[75] Ibid.

Montini suggests devoting the entire first session of the council to the theme of the church. In light of this focus, Montini argues that the council should begin by "turning its thoughts to Jesus Christ" for Christ is the principle of the church, since it is "both his emanation and his continuation."[76] As a way of underscoring the connection between Christ and the church, he urges that the council should, at its outset, "perform a unanimous and joyous act of homage, faithfulness, love and obedience to the Vicar of Christ."[77] Montini's certainty about the future council's focus on the church also acknowledges the historical precedent of Vatican I; he writes, "There were some defections, some hesitations and then some docile acceptances. Now the Church rejoices to recognize in Peter, in the person of his Successor, this fullness of powers which constitutes the secret of its unity, strength, and mysterious power to defy the times and make mankind into a 'Church.' Why not say so? Why does the Council not give expression to the certainty that has been achieved?"[78] Here, Montini shows that the connection between Vatican I and Vatican II is not only about the need to address the earlier council's limits and silences but also about building on its true achievements. After these important affirmations of Christ and the pope, Montini recommends concentrating on the mystery of the church, a topic that provides opportunity to elaborate and express doctrines concerning itself, including topics related to the laity, religious, bishops, and ecclesial life. He proposes concluding this first session with an extended deliberation among the bishops on the question "What is the Church?" It is this question, in Montini's mind, which represents John XXIII's original intention for the council because, in articulating an answer, the bishops can begin to express the place of the church in the modern world.

Montini advocates dedicating the council's second session to an examination of the church's mission. He notes, "All questions of morals, dogmas (related to the needs of our age, works of charity, missionary activity, etc.) would be studied in their due place

---

[76] Ibid.
[77] Ibid.
[78] Ibid., 103–4.

in this second stage of the council."[79] Following careful expression of the nature of the church, the council fathers could engage the question of mission and the work of evangelization which also informs its identity. Embracing Suenens's idea that the council should consider the church both *ad intra* and *ad extra*, Montini proposes that the third session focus on the relationship between the church and the world. This final session would look at many critical *ad extra* issues such as the church's relations with the economy, art, civil society, and enemies of the church. He recommends concluding the council with a celebration of the communion of saints and some charitable gesture which would "round off all the good words of the council with good deeds."[80] After outlining his ideas, Montini notes, "Perhaps all this is a fantasy, to be added to those that abound at this time of great spiritual ferment," yet sending these recommendations "spares me the remorse that would have come from keeping silent."[81]

The sense of a close connection between Vatican I's unfinished work and the development of Vatican II that was expressed by Suenens and Montini was also testified to by Karl Rahner, SJ. Reflecting on the council after its conclusion, Rahner noted:

> The "Church" was chosen as the central theme (of the Second Vatican Council) because of the fortuitous circumstance that this subject had been embarked upon on the First Vatican Council and then interrupted when that Council was prematurely broken off; and also because, as things are today, everywhere and in all the Churches and all the systems of theology belonging to them ecclesiology has come to be one of the most immediately relevant subjects of discussion, if not actually the primary subject.[82]

There is indisputable evidence that Vatican I's teachings served as an important horizon against which the shape and direction of

---

[79] Ibid., 104.

[80] Ibid.

[81] Ibid.

[82] Karl Rahner, "The New Image of the Church," in *Theological Investigations* 10 (New York: Seabury Press, 1977), 4.

Vatican II was formed. The fact that the <u>incomplete work of Vatican I was a critical starting point</u> for its successor's deliberations was taken for granted by many of the council's most influential figures. These leaders wanted to address Vatican I's unanswered questions while taking care to avoid its style, tone, and singular focus on papal authority. While there were differences regarding what impact Vatican I's teachings and silences should have on Vatican II's development, there was little doubt about the existence of a close relationship between the two councils.

IV. *Why* Vatican II Taught What It Taught

While in recent years considerable energy has been directed at examining the multiple historical and theological factors that shaped Vatican II, not enough attention has been paid to the way that Vatican I's teachings and silences served as one of the council's most critical contexts. The decisions and indecision of 1870 exerted formative influence not only on particular teachings at Vatican II but also on the shape of the council as a whole. To be sure, there were other historical and theological factors that significantly influenced Vatican II's agenda and its focus on local communities; Vatican II, however, cannot be completely understood apart from an awareness of its relation to its predecessor. In certain key ways, *why* Vatican II taught what it taught was to demonstrate continuity with its predecessor while answering the questions initially taken up, in limited fashion, at that earlier council.

The connection between Vatican I's legacy and the shape and success of Vatican II was not lost on many of the council fathers gathered by John XXIII in 1962. In fact, many leading voices, including Rahner, Congar, Suenens, Montini (Paul VI), and Schillebeeckx, explicitly identified maintaining continuity with Vatican I while bringing greater balance to its formulations as a foremost priority for the new council. These figures, who were contemporaneous with the council, did not feel the need to create distance between Vatican II and Vatican I in the way that some postconciliar scholars have done; instead, they were explicit about the necessity of a close connection between the two. Ignoring or rejecting Vatican I, however, certainly could have been an option. A council dedicated to seeking an enhanced relationship with the world and to *aggiornamento* could have easily articulated an explicit change in its content or relationship from that of its predecessor; the topic of papal infallibility offered an easy occasion for marking a break. In fact, such a rejection might have been a desirable way to seek favor with the world and advance dialogue with other Christians. Another possibility was that the upcoming council could ignore Vatican I completely, using its own silences to indicate discontinuity. The preparatory documents and the final texts of Vatican II could have avoided all mention of Vatican I as a way of politely yet clearly transmitting the message that what had transpired at the previous council was not representative of what the church really thought about these matters. Yet, in examining the development of Vatican II, it is clear that Vatican I's teachings and its silences are not avoided but instead engaged directly. This does not, by any means, indicate that the council fathers found Vatican I unproblematic or that they wanted to extend, replicate, or affirm all of its aspects. Rather, the preparatory stages for Vatican II demonstrate care to integrate elements of Vatican I's teachings with an awareness of the import of their contributions and also of their limitations. Doing so offered opportunities to fortify the conciliar tradition more generally and a coherent and persuasive vision of the church specifically.

Many observers, Catholics and non-Catholics alike, have lauded Vatican II for its shift to a more pastoral orientation and for its focus on episcopal authority, local communities, and the innate connections between the church's *ad intra* and *ad extra* dimensions. Praise for Vatican II's attention to these topics is oftentimes presented in contrast to the centralized view of the church presented by Vatican I with its more narrow focus on papal power and universal authority. Yet the choice of Vatican II's focus and direction did not fall out of the sky. Its orientation developed as the result of many factors. Critical among these was the lingering influence of the unfinished questions of Vatican I. In short, a key aspect of *why* Vatican II taught what it taught was that it needed to engage the critical silences of its predecessor and provide a proper contextualization for its teachings. The preparatory commentaries, *vota*, and plans which shaped the council demonstrate this engagement unambiguously. The decision to make the church and, in particular, the role of the bishop central topics within Vatican II's deliberations was not arrived at in ignorance of Vatican I's positions or its silences—nor as a refutation of them—but as a direct result of recognizing the need to attend to them. *Why* Vatican II was called cannot be understood apart from its relationship to Vatican I for, in many ways, *why* Vatican II taught what it taught was to provide more complete answers to questions that Vatican I had left unresolved.

Chapter Six

Vatican I's Impact on *What* and *How* Vatican II Taught

The new aspects of Vatican II were frequently stressed during and after the council. That there were such aspects is undeniable, but it is equally necessary to emphasize the conscious reality of continuity. . . . One clear example of this continuity is that the teaching of Vatican II about the episcopate and its collegiality is thought to have restored equilibrium to the purely papal emphasis of Vatican I, as Paul VI declared on two occasions (29 November and 21 December 1963) that it ought to do. The continuity between the two councils was demonstrated by the evidence that the teaching of Vatican II had already been sketched out in the plans of Vatican I.[1]

—Yves Congar, OP

Vatican II's direction and development were shaped by an effort to bring greater balance to its predecessor's teachings. This desire is underscored in the writings of many of the key architects of the council, including John XXIII, Paul VI, Congar, Suenens, and Rahner, who all acknowledged a critical relationship between Vatican II's agenda and the unfinished work of Vatican I. The impact of Vatican I's legacy on *why* Vatican II taught what it taught was examined in the previous chapter. The present chapter will

---

[1] Yves Congar, "A Last Look at the Council," in *Vatican II Revisited by Those Who Were There*, ed. Albert Stacpoole (Minneapolis, MN: Winston Press, 1986), 337–58, at 341.

examine other critical links between the two councils by exploring ways that Vatican I influenced *how* and *what* Vatican II taught on the topic of ecclesial authority, specifically in *Lumen Gentium* 18–23.

Lumen Gentium, Vatican II's Dogmatic Constitution on the Church, was promulgated on November 21, 1964, during the council's third session.[2] Even though it was not the first text taken up or approved by the council fathers, discussions on the church played a prominent role in the council's preparatory stages and initial sessions. The original preparatory schema on the church, *De Ecclesia*, which the council fathers received on November 23, 1962, reflected much of the institutional and juridical character that many hoped the council would supersede.[3] The text began with a chapter on the church militant and was, overall, "marked by the defensive preoccupation with church structures that had shaped the official church teaching since the Reformation."[4] In the bishops' debates on the schema during the first session, a majority of bishops expressed dissatisfaction, arguing that it failed to represent the vision for the council laid out by John XXIII. Their interventions indicated that they wanted the council's consideration of the church to be, among other things, more biblical, more ecumenical, more liturgical, and more Christocentric.[5] This led to massive work during the intersession to produce a substantially revised text. When the council resumed in September 1963, a second schema was presented which reflected a significant development: instead of focusing on the church militant, the first chapter now presented the church as mystery. This shift to speaking of the

[2] Two important sources for understanding the history and theology of *Lumen Gentium* include "Dogmatic Constitution on the Church," in *Commentary on the Documents of Vatican II*, vol. 1, ed. Herbert Vorgrimmler (New York: Herder and Herder, 1966); and Richard Gaillardetz, *The Church in the Making:* Lumen Gentium, Christus Dominus, Orientalium Ecclesiarum (New York: Paulist Press, 2006).

[3] For more on the first draft of the schema and its reception, see Giuseppe Ruggieri, "Beyond an Ecclesiology of Polemics: The Debate on the Church," in Alberigo and Komonchak, *History of Vatican II*, 2:281–358.

[4] Hahnenberg, *A Concise Guide to the Documents of Vatican II*, 39.

[5] See Komonchak, "The Significance of Vatican Council II for Ecclesiology," 72–83.

church in its spiritual dimensions constituted an effort to retrieve elements of the early church's understanding. A third draft of the schema, discussed during the council's third session, further embraced this orientation with the addition of a chapter on the people of God and expanded considerations of holiness and eschatology. At the end of the deliberations on the schema, Pope Paul VI included an Explanatory Note (*Nota Explicative Praevia*) intended to placate a minority of bishops who opposed the document; however, some feared that his accommodations contradicted the spirit of the text.[6] After many successive revisions and explanations which shifted the council's presentation of the church into increasingly theological and aspirational language, the bishops approved *Lumen Gentium* with a vote of 2,151 to 5.

Even with an awareness of the influence that Vatican I exerted in shaping the questions of Vatican II, the extent of *Lumen Gentium*'s reliance on *Pastor Aeternus* can remain somewhat surprising. While it became inevitable that Vatican II would continue a conversation initiated by Vatican I, it was not inevitable, nor necessary, that the council would explicitly affirm or rely on its predecessor's decrees. In fact, any affirmation of Vatican I's teachings might be seen as distinctly unlikely, given that much of the interest in the council resulted from dissatisfaction with its unbalanced presentation of authority. While Vatican I's formulations, as formal doctrine, could not be contradicted by Vatican II, it might be assumed that they would not be engaged. Put another way, one might expect the one-sidedness of Vatican I's depiction of centralized authority to be mirrored by its successor in a one-sided focus on local authority. *Lumen Gentium* reveals that this is not the case; on the contrary, the text explicitly affirms *Pastor Aeternus*'s position on papal authority and takes it as a key starting point in its own teachings on the origin and nature of the bishops' office. *Lumen Gentium*'s point of departure thus suggests notable convergence on the very subject—authority—which is often portrayed as the point of opposition between the councils.

---

[6] For the controversy over Paul VI's Explanatory Note, see Luis Antonio Tagle, "The Black Week of Vatican II (November 14–21, 1964)," in Alberigo and Komonchak, *History of Vatican II*, 3:417–44.

On examination, *Lumen Gentium*'s connections to *Pastor Aeternus*'s teachings—and *Pastor Aeternus*'s silences—become clear, even to those who wish they were not there. In all, *Lumen Gentium* makes thirty-nine references to the texts of previous councils. Of these, thirteen, or one-third, are references to Vatican I. This far exceeds references to any other council save Trent, which is also referenced thirteen times.[7] In its third chapter, dedicated to ecclesial authority, *Lumen Gentium*'s reliance on Vatican I is particularly striking. In this chapter, previous councils are cited twenty-four times and, of those, nine are appeals to Vatican I. The reliance on Vatican I becomes even more pronounced if one notes that in addition to those nine references to the council's documents, there are also seven references to commentaries on the council written by Gasser, Bishop Federico Maria Zinelli, and Bishop Josef Wilhelm Karl Kluetgen.[8] The connection between *Lumen Gentium* and *Pastor Aeternus* indicates, from the outset, that Vatican II sought to build on the teachings of Vatican I rather than reject or radically reconfigure them.

As we have seen, many of the bishops and theologians involved in the development of Vatican II felt that numerous affirmations of Vatican I were necessary in order to demonstrate continuity between the councils. This was especially important for some at Vatican II who worried that the council's support of episcopal collegiality would be seen as inconsistent with what had been taught about the papacy at Vatican I. Some postconciliar commentators, however, have lamented the extent of *Lumen Gentium*'s affirmations of *Pastor Aeternus*, arguing that it creates a kind of schizophrenia in the text. These observers claim that attempts to

---

[7] This means that twenty-six of *Lumen Gentium*'s thirty-nine references to previous councils, or two-thirds, are references to one of Vatican II's two most immediate predecessors. While it is clear that Vatican II seeks to retrieve elements of the church's early tradition, the numerous citations of Trent and Vatican I demonstrate that these more recent councils can also be seen as consistent with the teachings of the universal church. The references reflect the way that *Lumen Gentium* attempts to integrate ecclesiological principles from the first and second millennia.

[8] Zinelli, "*Relatio* on Vatican Council I," is found in Mansi 52, 1109–14. Kleutgen, "Commentary on Vatican I," appears in Mansi 53, 313 AB.

integrate the juridical elements of Vatican I hinder *Lumen Gentium's* ability to advance the more sacramental and biblically based vision of the church that the majority of bishops desired.[9] Massimo Faggioli, for instance, argues that *Lumen Gentium's* efforts to integrate its vision of authority with that of Vatican I restricts it from reflecting the full ecclesiological vision of the council fathers. He argues that such a vision is better achieved in *Sacrosanctum Concilium,* Vatican II's Constitution on the Liturgy, which is "less compromised by the need to redeem or correct the trajectories of the recent past of nineteenth- and early twentieth-century ecclesiology."[10] Given that *Lumen Gentium's* reliance on *Pastor Aeternus* is clear, the question is not whether there is a close relationship between these two texts; rather, the question concerns *how* Vatican I influences Vatican II and whether their positions can be fruitfully reconciled. Examining the nature of the continuity between *Pastor Aeternus* and *Lumen Gentium*—where it exists and on what topics—illumines the character and value of their relationship.

Exploring elements of continuity and complementarity in the teachings of Vatican I and Vatican II is best accomplished through a close reading of *Lumen Gentium* 18–23, which relies on *Pastor Aeternus* most directly. Both the form of *Lumen Gentium's* presentation, *how* it teaches, and the content of its presentation, *what* it teaches, are significantly influenced by the earlier constitution. The nature and origin of episcopal authority and its relation to the papacy are extremely complex topics and ones which, on their own merits, warrant multivolume studies. Keeping in mind the narrower question of the relationship between Vatican I and Vatican II, this chapter addresses two particular questions—one related to continuity in the form of *Lumen Gentium* and *Pastor Aeternus* and the other to complementarity in their content. The chapter will begin by asking: *how* does *Lumen Gentium* make its

---

[9] See Massimo Fagiolli, *True Reform: Liturgy and Ecclesiology in Sacrosanctum Concilium* (Collegeville, MN: Liturgical Press, 2012).

[10] Faggioli, *True Reform*, 80.

argument regarding the origin and nature of episcopal authority? It will then consider: *what* does *Lumen Gentium* say about the nature of episcopal authority and its relationship to papal authority? Exploring these questions demonstrates that Vatican I and Vatican II not only share many of the same questions but also share critical answers and styles of presentation.

I. The Third Chapter of *Lumen Gentium*: *How* It Teaches on Ecclesial Authority

The third chapter of *Lumen Gentium* addresses many of the most urgent silences of Vatican I. In regard to this chapter, Rahner remarked that "the moment had come to speak of something which Vatican I had already recognized as a task still to be completed. . . . It was essential to speak of the nature and of the office of the episcopate as a whole."[11] This chapter treats questions regarding the origin and role of the bishop and the relationship between episcopal and papal authority while being careful not to oversimplify these realities. Because the third chapter of *Lumen Gentium* addresses the subject matter of many of the most contentious debates at Vatican I, it has the greatest potential for conflict with the texts of that council. Yet, as will be shown, many elements of the chapter's style and subject matter reflect an eagerness to maintain continuity with *Pastor Aeternus* while simultaneously seeking to go beyond it.

Turning first to the question regarding *how* Vatican II presents its view of the episcopate, a close study of *Lumen Gentium* 18–23 demonstrates that its treatment of authority mirrors, in several key ways, *Pastor Aeternus*'s presentation of this topic. The similarities between the two constitutions begin even with their titles. Both Vatican I's *Pastor Aeternus* ("Eternal Shepherd") and Vatican II's *Lumen Gentium* ("Light of the Nations") have titles that are names for Christ. These two constitutions on the church, notably the only two constitutions in the entire conciliar tradition

---

[11] Karl Rahner, "The Hierarchical Structure of the Church, With Special Reference to the Episcopate," in *Commentary on the Documents of Vatican II*, ed. Herbert Vorgrimmler, vol. 1 (New York: Herder and Herder, 1967–1969), 187.

on this theme, both begin with a reference to Christ rather than to the church itself. This choice affirms the reality that the church is not an end in itself but points beyond itself to Christ, who serves as its source and constitutes its unity. In their initial discussions on the church, the council fathers at Vatican II cited the words of St. Augustine: "Through his Church he (Christ) comes to the nations and through the Church he speaks to the nations."[12] These words, in many ways, capture the reform envisaged by the council—to make the church more transparent to Christ.[13] Another motivation for the christological starting points in these texts is the desire to demonstrate continuity with the patrimony of the ancient church which had always maintained a close connection between these loci. By beginning with Christ, both texts seek to avoid the impression that their teachings are innovative or radically separate from the heart of the Gospel message or the witness of the church's universal tradition. This allows them to respond to urgent contemporary questions while remaining firmly rooted in the tradition of Christian history. Thus, a key aspect of *how* both *Pastor Aeternus* and *Lumen Gentium* approach the issue of ecclesial authority is that each, beginning with their very titles, roots its presentation of the church in Christ as a way to theologically and historically contextualize its teachings.

Lumen Gentium begins its discussion of episcopal authority with an explicit affirmation of *Pastor Aeternus*. It states, "This holy synod, following in the steps of the first Vatican Council, with it teaches and declares that Jesus Christ, the eternal pastor, established the holy church by sending the apostles as he himself had been sent by the Father (cf. Jn. 20:21)" (LG 18). Not only does this opening passage declare that the constitution follows "in the footsteps" of its predecessor; it also refers to Christ as the "eternal pastor," an allusion to *Pastor Aeternus*. This reference to Christ as "eternal pastor" anchors the theme of the chapter. It conveys that the guidance and stability Christ provides to the apostles in their mission is the same support that the bishops receive in their continuation of that mission. That Vatican II's long-awaited treatment

---

[12] Aloys Grillmeier, "The Mystery of the Church," in *Commentary on the Documents of Vatican II*, 1:138–52, at 139.

[13] Ibid.

of local authority begins with multiple references to Vatican I, rather than an attempt to distance itself from the previous council, sets a clear tone and foundation for the document. Regarding these allusions early in the text, Rahner notes, "The link between the chapter on the bishops and the dogmatic definition of authority of the Pope in Vatican I was universally welcomed. . . . It was not a matter of contrasting two rival powers, but of describing an organic union, unique in its kind, which links the supreme head of the Church hierarchy with the bishops as a group."[14] This link was welcomed not only as a means of affirming Vatican I's teaching but also as a way of freeing *Lumen Gentium* from distracting debates regarding whether what was being said did or did not compromise the definitions of 1870.[15]

Lumen Gentium moves quickly to the theme of Christian unity and the way that it constitutes the goal and character of ecclesial authority. In turning to this topic, the text begins by repeating almost verbatim a passage from *Pastor Aeternus*. *Lumen Gentium* states, "In order that the episcopate itself, however, might be one and undivided he [Christ] placed blessed Peter over the other apostles, and in him he set up a lasting and visible source and foundation of the unity both of faith and of communion" (LG 18). This affirmation mirrors the first chapter of *Pastor Aeternus* which asserts, "In order that the episcopate itself would be one and undivided and that, by means of a close union among the priests, the whole multitude of believers should be maintained in the unity of faith and communion, He [Christ] set blessed Peter over the rest of the apostles and instituted in him a permanent principle of both unities and their visible foundation" (PA 1). *Lumen Gentium's* move from Christ to unity to authority mirrors that of *Pastor Aeternus's* structure which sets the prerogatives of the pope in this same context. Both texts describe ecclesial authority not as a means

---

[14] Rahner, "The Hierarchical Structure of the Church," 113.

[15] Despite Rahner's observation that *Lumen Gentium's* early references to Vatican I were "universally welcomed," not everyone would agree with this assessment. Küng calls this affirmation of Vatican I at the beginning of *Lumen Gentium* a "massive endorsement"; he ultimately considers it "hollow praise," however, in that he sees nearly everything that follows it as representing an effort to overcome problems created by Pius IX's council. See Küng, *Infallible?*, 56–71.

of domination but as a type of assistance given to the whole church which is exercised by particular leaders. They show Christ as endowing Peter with an authority intended to unite the apostles and, through them, the entire Christian community. This gift of authority is communicated to the pope, as the successor to Peter, and to the bishops, as the successor to the apostles, for this same end. Thus, *how Lumen Gentium* links the themes of Christ, authority, and unity as a way of introducing its teaching on episcopal authority is not its own innovation but follows the same pattern as its predecessor. The fact that Vatican II mirrors Vatican I in the way it roots its teaching on ecclesial authority provides strong evidence of the way that it saw itself as building on the work of its predecessor.

As *Lumen Gentium* moves into its articulation of the character of episcopal power, additional similarities between its form and the form of *Pastor Aeternus* emerge. In fact, *Lumen Gentium*'s treatment of the origin and exercise of the papacy represents an exact parallel with *Pastor Aeternus*'s treatment of the origin and exercise of the papacy and its authority. *Pastor Aeternus* begins its first chapter by discussing the divine institution of primacy in Peter. This is immediately followed in the second chapter with the assertion that the bishop of Rome is successor to Peter in the ministry of the primacy. More important, the same sequence of topics is maintained in *Lumen Gentium*. *Lumen Gentium* 19 affirms the divine institution of the college of apostles. Directly after this, *Lumen Gentium* 20 teaches that the college of bishops is the successor to the college of the apostles. *Pastor Aeternus* presents its argument for the origin and exercise of papal primacy by demonstrating that Peter is chosen by Christ as head of the church and that Christ has willed that this divinely instituted office would function in an unbroken line of succession; *Lumen Gentium* structures its argument for episcopal authority similarly.[16] This is clear in *Lumen Gentium* 20, which states,

---

[16] William Henn discusses this parallel sequencing in his book *The Honor of My Brothers: A Brief History of the Relationship between the Pope and the Bishops* (New York: Crossroad, 2000). See especially the chapter titled "Vatican II: Communion, Collegiality and Primacy," 143–57.

> *Just as* the office which the Lord confided to Peter personally, as first of the apostles, is permanent, intended to be transmitted to his successors, *so too* is the office of which the apostles received as pastors of the church, a task destined to be exercised without interruption by the sacred order of bishops. The sacred synod consequently teaches that the bishops have by divine institution taken the place of the apostles as pastors of the church in such wise that whoever hears them hears Christ and whoever rejects them rejects Christ and him who sent Christ. (LG 20, emphasis added)

This *"just as," "so too"* mode of argument is utilized in multiple places in *Lumen Gentium*. We see above that *"just as"* Christ endows Peter with authority that is transmitted in unbroken succession, *"so too"* does Christ endow the apostles, and their successors, the bishops, with authority. Similarly, paragraph 22 states that *"just as*, in accordance with the Lord's decree, St Peter and the other apostles constitute one apostolic college, *so [too]* in like fashion the Roman Pontiff, Peter's successor, and the bishops, the successors of the apostles, are joined together" (LG 22). Throughout *Lumen Gentium*, the character of papal authority, as it is presented in *Pastor Aeternus*, is offered as a primary warrant for its position on episcopal authority. The fact that *Lumen Gentium* adopts important aspects not just of *Pastor Aeternus*'s content but also its form shows an acceptance of Vatican I's position *and* its rationale. This represents a stronger degree of affirmation than would be reflected in merely repeating its content. The replication of Vatican I's style and line of argument suggests that the bishops at Vatican II saw themselves as extending the work of that earlier constitution by applying its argument to their consideration of episcopal authority.

The parallels in form between *Pastor Aeternus* and *Lumen Gentium* are significant on multiple levels and provide a critical lens for the interpretation of both councils. Certainly these parallels reveal important things regarding the proper interpretation of Vatican II; *Lumen Gentium*'s use of *Pastor Aeternus*, however, also speaks to the proper interpretation of Vatican I. In its reliance on *Pastor Aeternus*, *Lumen Gentium* engages in a critical re-reading and re-reception of that earlier constitution. The opening paragraphs of *Pastor Aeternus* establish a context that is critical for interpreting its teaching on papal authority; this is often over-looked. As was seen previously in chapter 3, the initial paragraphs of *Pastor Aeternus* contextualize papal infallibility within the horizons of the church's universal tradition and a more comprehensive ecclesiology. In particular, they highlight the inherently relational character of the papacy and the way that promoting ecclesial unity is constitutive of its nature. Yet, these opening paragraphs are often ignored, and the definition of papal infallibility, which appears at the end of the constitution, is read in isolation. This type of noncontextual reading "distorts" *Pastor Aeternus* and obscures the way that *Lumen Gentium* "is actually a legitimate development and not a repudiation of the fundamental direction" set by Vatican I.[17] By mirroring the form of *Pastor Aeternus* and adopting the contextualizing features of its early paragraphs, *Lumen Gentium* directs attention to the way that *Pastor Aeternus*'s presentation of papal authority must be seen in the context of the whole document. In this way, *Lumen Gentium* calls for a re-reading of papal infallibility that situates this authority within a wider understanding of the papacy and ultimately a wider understanding of the church. Therefore, *Lumen Gentium*'s embrace of certain aspects of *Pastor Aeternus*'s form serves a dual purpose: first, it affirms the importance of the relational character of the *episcopacy* and the way that this character shapes the proper exercise of episcopal authority. Second, it affirms the relational character of the *papacy* and the way that its authority must be seen in a broad context. Ultimately, by repeating key aspects of Vatican I's form, Vatican II is not only offering its own teaching on ecclesial authority but also interpreting its predecessor's as well.

Another critical aspect of the way that Vatican II engages in a re-reading of Vatican I is found in *how* the later council engages the teachings of the earlier one. To establish continuity with Vatican I, *Lumen Gentium* relies not only on the council's final documents but also on other critical commentaries by Gasser, Zinnelli, and Kleutegen. For example, in order to deny that Vatican I espouses a view of papal infallibility as personal, *Lumen Gentium* 25 cites

---

[17] Buckley, *Papal Primacy and the Episcopate*, 45.

Gasser's *relatio* on this issue. It adopts Gasser's statement that "the Roman Pontiff does not utter a pronouncement as a private person, but rather does he expound and defend the teaching of the Catholic faith as the supreme teacher of the universal Church, in whom the Church's charism of infallibility is present in a singular way."[18] Thus, *Lumen Gentium* refutes the notion that *Pastor Aeternus* advocates an extreme notion of the pope's infallibility as personal, not by pointing to that text, but by pointing to Gasser's explanation of it. The use of Gasser indicates that this limit on the pope's authority is not clear from the letter of Vatican I's documents but is clear in light of other contextualizing factors beyond the documents themselves.[19] *Lumen Gentium*'s choice to invoke Gasser's interpretation reflects the reality that the meaning of conciliar teachings is understood not only by examining the final texts themselves but also by seeing those texts within their proper context and as part of a larger tradition. Thus, *how* Vatican II presents Vatican I's teaching indicates something regarding *how* the earlier council's texts should be read.

II. The Third Chapter of *Lumen Gentium*: What It Teaches on Ecclesial Authority

Turning now to *what* Vatican II teaches regarding ecclesial authority. A close examination of *Pastor Aeternus* and *Lumen Gentium* reveals striking complementarity in the content of their teachings, some aspects of which have already been glimpsed in the discussion above regarding *how* Vatican II taught on the topic of episcopal authority. Upon examining *Lumen Gentium*'s third chapter, it becomes clear that *what* it teaches often intends to fill one or

---

[18] *Lumen Gentium* cites Gasser's text from J. D. Mansi, 52:1213.

[19] It is important to clarify that Gasser's *relatio* is not completely independent from Vatican I in that it was developed in the course of the council by Gasser as part of the *Disputation De fide*. It remains, however, that the *relatio* is an interpretation of the council's definition on papal infallibility that is not part of the final documents. This highlights that Vatican I's final texts are not seen as self-interpreting, but there are interpretive contexts in which its meaning gets mediated.

more of Vatican I's silences. Chapter 3 of *Lumen Gentium* focuses explicitly on episcopal authority; its full title indicates this intent: "The Hierarchical Structure of the Church, with Special Reference to the Episcopate." The wisdom of the chapter's "special reference to the episcopate" can only be appreciated in light of the context set by Vatican I. As we have seen, Vatican I's unanswered questions oriented Vatican II's to the theme of the church. The earlier council, however, was not entirely silent on this topic. Vatican I taught in a definitive way regarding some aspects of papal authority, but it did not substantively address matters related to episcopal authority. Therefore, what Vatican I conferred on its successor was never received as an undifferentiated interest in ecclesiology but a particular focus on questions related to local authority. Apart from Vatican I's legacy, Vatican II's focus on the church's hierarchy "with special reference to the episcopate" makes no sense; instead, it also seems like a one-sided or limited conversation. It is precisely because of Vatican I's teachings that Vatican II's reflection on the church acquired this "special accent of its own."[20]

At the center of *what* Vatican II taught about episcopal power and its relation to papal power lie two related claims. First is the sacramental nature of the episcopacy and second is the notion of episcopal collegiality. Both of these issues engage important silences in Vatican I's texts. At the heart of *Lumen Gentium's* discussion of ecclesial authority is an affirmation of a sacramental basis of the episcopal office. The text teaches that the bishops receive special gifts of the Holy Spirit at their ordination in order to fulfill their primary role as shepherds of God's people by maintaining order and unity among them. The key passage on this point is worth quoting at length:

> In order to fulfil such exalted functions, the apostles were endowed by Christ with a special outpouring of the holy Spirit coming upon

---

[20] This comment was made by Paul VI on September 14, 1964, in his opening address at the third session of the council. In reflecting on the pope's words, Gerard Philips notes that Paul VI understood that "the Second Vatican Council was completing the First, which had done all it could to work out the definition of the functions and power of the Pope." See Gerard Philips, "The History of the Constitution," in *Commentary on the Documents of Vatican II*, 1:105–37, at 126.

them, and, by the imposition of hands they passed on to their col-
laborators the gift of the Spirit, which is transmitted down to our
day through episcopal consecration. The holy Synod teaches, moreover, that the fullness of the Sacrament of Orders is conferred by
episcopal consecration, that fullness, namely, which both in the
liturgical tradition of the church and in the language of the Fathers
of the church is called the high priesthood, the summit of the sacred
ministry. Episcopal consecration confers, together with the office of
sanctifying, the offices also of teaching and ruling, which, however,
of their very nature can be exercised only in hierarchical communion
with the head and members of the college. (LG 21)

The declaration that the authority exercised by the episcopacy,
with its roles of teaching, sanctifying, and governing, is communicated by episcopal consecration put to rest a debate that had
been a matter of controversy for centuries in the church, namely,
whether episcopal jurisdiction comes immediately from the pope
or comes through episcopal consecration and, thus, immediately
from Christ. It also excluded a view advanced by several scholastic
theologians that there was no sacramental difference between a
priest and a bishop. *Lumen Gentium*'s teaching about the sacramental character of the bishops' powers is critical in that, in addition to resolving an issue that had been considered an open
question for several hundred years, it reflects a shift from viewing
the character of episcopal authority predominately in juridical
terms to considering it fundamentally in its sacramental, ontological reality. The importance and distinction of this development
was highlighted by Congar, who remarked that "the only passage
of the Dogmatic Constitution on the Church which could be considered as a true and proper dogmatic declaration is that which
concerns the sacramentality of the episcopacy."[21]

What Vatican II teaches regarding the sacramental character of
episcopal authority provides not only a complement to Vatican I's
position but also adds necessary contextualization to it. *Pastor
Aeternus* affirmed the episcopal character of the papacy, noting
that "the Roman church possesses a pre-eminence of ordinary

---

[21] See Yves Congar, "*In luogo di conclusion*," in *La Chiesa del Vaticano II*, ed.
G. Barauna (Florence: Vallecchi, 1965), 1262.

power over every other church; and that this jurisdictional power
of the Roman pontiff is both episcopal and immediate" (PA 3).
This affirmation was underscored in Zinelli's important *relatio* on
the text which states, "It must be admitted that the power of the
sovereign pontiff is in reality of the same type as that of the
bishops. Why then not use the same word to describe the quality
of jurisdiction exercised by the pope and by the bishops, and why
not say that episcopal power resides in the bishops and the supreme episcopal power in the sovereign pontiff."[22] While Vatican
I makes these assertions about the episcopal character of the papacy, it does not describe the nature of the episcopacy and thus
the character of that shared power. This lacunae means that despite the fact that Vatican I clearly defines certain aspects of the
pope's power, it remains that the nature of this office is "insufficiently understood" given that it cannot be fully appreciated apart
from a rich understanding of the episcopacy.[23] Thus, the fact that
Vatican II clarifies critical elements of the episcopate, such as its
sacramental character, not only advances its own aims but also
supplies critical contextualization to Vatican I's presentation of
the papacy.

After treating the sacramental nature of the episcopacy, *Lumen
Gentium* moves directly into a discussion of episcopal collegiality,
or the way in which the bishops work together with the pope as
their head in exercising their responsibility for the church. This
topic, according to Rahner, "is one of the central themes of the
whole Council."[24] *Lumen Gentium* states that the authority

---

[22] Quoted in Buckley, *Papal Primacy and the Episcopate*, 59. Also notable is that
the notion that the service of the primacy is an episcopal service is a key theme
of John Paul II's *Ut Unum Sint*. The encyclical notes: "The Catholic Church does
not separate this office from the mission entrusted to the whole body of
bishops. . . . This service of unity, rooted in the action of divine mercy, is entrusted within the college of bishops to one among those who have received
from the Spirit this task, not the exercising of power over people—as the rulers
of the gentiles and their great men do (cf. Matt 20:25; Mark 10:42)—but of leading them towards peaceful pastures" (par. 94).

[23] Buckley develops this point in his chapter "The Episcopal Character of Papal
Primacy," in *Papal Primacy and the Episcopate*, 59–61.

[24] Rahner, "The Hierarchical Structure of the Church," 195.

conferred to bishops in their ordination incorporates them into the college of bishops. In fact, the authority of their office "can be exercised only in hierarchical communion with the head and members of the college" (LG 21). As such, the exercise of the sacramentally based authority of the episcopate is necessarily situated within the context of a college composed of head and members. The fact that these topics are linked so closely—the sacramental nature of the episcopacy and the existence of the episcopal college—shows that, for the fathers at Vatican II, the idea of an episcopal college serves as the framework that provides the proper perspective for understanding all aspects of the episcopacy.

Lumen Gentium 22 serves as the key paragraph on the character of the episcopal college. It begins, significantly, with an affirmation of the pope's authority. Reiterating Vatican I's teaching, the text states, "The Roman Pontiff, by reason of his office as Vicar of Christ and as pastor of the entire church, has full, supreme and universal power over the whole church, a power which he can exercise freely" (LG 22). After affirming the pope's primacy, it then asserts that the bishops also have responsibility for the whole church and exercise their own proper authority for the good of their faithful, indeed even for the good of the whole church" (LG 22). In this paragraph, the council fathers make the critical affirmation that "together with its head, the Supreme Pontiff, and never apart from him, it [the college of bishops] is the subject of supreme and full authority over the universal Church; but this power cannot be exercised without the consent of the Roman Pontiff" (LG 22). Thus, Vatican II's teaching on collegiality is rooted in an idea of shared authority between the pope and bishops. Edward Hahnenberg points out that *Lumen Gentium* sees authority passing to Peter and the apostles together. This authority is then passed to the whole college of bishops, with the pope as its head.[25] By affirming the bishops' responsibility for the whole church and placing the pope within the college, Vatican II moves beyond a deeply entrenched tendency to view the bishops' authority and the pope's authority competitively in the manner of a zero-sum game.[26] The council

---

[25] Hahnenberg, *A Concise Guide to the Documents of Vatican II*, 46.
[26] See Gaillardetz and Clifford, *Keys to the Council*, 124–27.

seeks to retrieve the *communio* model of the first millennium which viewed the church as a communion of churches and situate Vatican I's teaching on the papacy in that context. It thus establishes collegiality as a primary lens for viewing all authority in the church. Here again, Vatican II's efforts to advance its own teachings includes a helpful re-reading and related interpretation of its predecessor's positions.

The emphasis on the sacramental and collegial nature of episcopal power clarifies that the bishops are not vicars of the pope but heads of particular churches. *Just as* the pope serves as the visible principle of unity for the whole church, *so too* do the bishops serve as visible principles of unity for each local church. *Lumen Gentium* 23 states:

> Individual bishops are the visible source and foundation of unity in their own particular churches, which are modelled on the universal church; it is in and from these that the one and unique catholic church exists. And for that reason each bishop represents his own church, whereas all of them together with the pope represent the whole church in a bond of peace, love and unity. (LG 23)

Lumen Gentium here retrieves the ancient notion that each particular church is "wholly church, but not the whole church."[27] Individual dioceses are not outposts of Rome; they are communities where the whole mystery of Christ is present and realized. Such a vision further supports collegiality, "for each bishop represents his own church and, together with the pope, all bishops represent the whole church."[28] These declarations made in support of the bishop's authority had the additional effect of retrieving the theological significance of local churches.[29] Recognizing the authority of local bishops gives theological warrant for the existence of diverse expressions of the Gospel within local churches. Vatican II's attention to local and diverse expressions of the Gospel, in many ways, became another "special accent" of Vatican II's teachings.

---

[27] Hahnenberg, *A Concise Guide to the Documents of Vatican II*, 47.
[28] Ibid.
[29] Komonchak, "The Significance of Vatican Council II for Ecclesiology," 80–81.

Vatican II, from the very beginning, recognized the need to provide a "necessary complement" to Vatican I's positions on papal primacy and infallibility.[30] This meant that it had the "delicate task" of balancing its views on episcopal power with its predecessor's teachings on papal power.[31] A central question before the bishops at Vatican II, therefore, was how these two authorities should be seen in relation to one another and who, ultimately, serves as the "court of last resort" in the church. *Lumen Gentium* is clear that there are two subjects of supreme authority in the church—the college of bishops and the pope, acting as the head of the college. *Lumen Gentium* succeeds in providing some degree of greater clarity to the relationship between episcopal power and papal power by affirming *what* Vatican I taught and complementing it with a robust view of episcopal authority. In many ways, however, *Lumen Gentium*'s treatment of this issue raises more questions than it answers. Rahner speaks to the tension inherent in *Lumen Gentium*'s treatment of this issue; he writes:

> It is difficult to determine the exact relationship between the Pope acting as primate and the college of bishops along with the Pope (including his special function *within* the college). Here the text leaves questions open. It merely repeats the doctrine of the primacy given by Vatican I, and then affirms that a college of bishops and its collegiate act cannot exist without the Pope as head and without his special co-operation with the collegiate act. The relationship is hard to determine, because the Pope "alone" (*seorsim*) has the same full and supreme authority over the Church (including all the individual bishops) as the college of bishops as a whole.[32]

Rahner identifies a critical silence in *Lumen Gentium*; that is, even as the constitution fully affirms papal authority and its freedom to act, it vests a fullness of authority in the college of bishops without specifying the mechanics of these two subjects of power. It does not, for instance, describe how these two subjects of supreme authority exercise their respective prerogatives in every instance

---

[30] Ibid., 86.

[31] Ibid.

[32] Rahner, "The Hierarchical Structure of the Church," 201.

and, especially, in moments of disagreement. Thus, while *Lumen Gentium* advances the question of the exercise of ecclesial authority, it remains incomplete, such that practical and theological questions linger. Again, Rahner speaks to the heart of the matter:

> Why, for instance, is it not a contradiction to hold that in the same society there are (at least apparently) two different possessors of the same full and supreme power, without destroying the unity of the society or (at least implicitly) denying supreme power to one or other of the claimants (as, for instance, when the college of its council is said to derive its power from the Pope as primate of the Church?) And again, in practice, is not the initiative and free authority of the college reduced to a mere fiction, if the pope is always "free" to repress its activities?[33]

Lumen Gentium does not provide clear juridical parameters to deal with critical issues related to the relationship between the pope and the bishops; instead, as Rahner says, "The text leaves questions open."[34] Here, we see that Vatican II has its own silences, vital issues which it leaves unresolved in order to allow space for ongoing development and contextualization.

"Open questions" and unresolved juxtapositions, however, often illumine truth in profound ways. One reality that is illumined is *how* the council fathers at Vatican II approached the episcopacy. Vatican II presents the relations between these two subjects—the pope and the episcopal college—in a theological manner rather than a juridical one. Interestingly, the word *iurisdictio*, which appears frequently in the relatively short four chapters of *Pastor Aeternus* (seven times), is found only rarely within all sixteen of Vatican II's documents (nine times). *Lumen Gentium's* limited use of this term suggests that the idea of jurisdiction was not the lens that dominated the council fathers' thinking about the episcopacy. Instead, they sought to treat ecclesial authority from a sacramental and ontological perspective and, as such, were content to present elements of the episcopacy and its relation to the papacy without feeling the need to resolve every tension and

---

[33] Ibid.
[34] Ibid.

synthesize every position, particularly those of particular rights and jurisdiction. Therefore, according to Komonchak, "Rather than offering a speculative resolution of the difficulty, the council was content to set out terms that any such theory must take into account."[35] Ultimately, *what* Vatican II taught on the bishops was not meant to be taken as a final word but the start of a conversation.

III. Mutually Interpreting Councils

How and *what* Vatican II taught on the subject of ecclesial authority were shaped by its efforts to maintain continuity with Vatican I and bring a higher level of completion to its teachings. In both form and content, Vatican II is clear in affirming Vatican I's presentation of the papacy and takes it as a basis for its own teachings. *How* Vatican II presents the topic of ecclesial authority, in several critical ways, relies on the manner in which Vatican I engaged this topic. Vatican II adopts elements of Vatican I's argument and form which indicates the later council's support for the positions of the earlier one as well as aspects of its rationale. *What* Vatican II taught is also profoundly influenced by Vatican I. The content of Vatican II's treatment of ecclesial authority is often the exact subject matter of the silences of its predecessor. Vatican II's focus on episcopal authority as "its special accent" is largely derived from its desire to balance and complete the unfinished work of its predecessor.

Certainly, Vatican II's efforts to balance the more juridical and centralized model of Vatican I with its retrieval of elements of the *communio* model of the first millennium is not without its challenges. This difficulty is evident in the way that *Lumen Gentium* merely juxtaposes its positions with those of *Pastor Aeternus* without fully reconciling them. It remains, however, that these two dimensions of the church's life—the juridical and the theological— are both critical and exist simultaneously. They are difficult to integrate but must be integrated. At some level, this intentional

---

[35] Komonchak, "The Significance of Vatican Council II for Ecclesiology," 87.

effort by *Lumen Gentium* and the council fathers ought to be received as part of the council's spirit and ecclesiological vision. Vatican II seeks to transcend a narrow lens which sets papal authority and episcopal authority in a competitive relationship. This means that, rather than choosing *either* Vatican I's strong view of papal authority *or* Vatican II's robust notion of episcopal collegiality, those receiving the councils must work to understand these authorities—and thus the conciliar agendas—together. It is precisely those aspects of ecclesial authority that Vatican II was not able to fully reconcile which presents the postconciliar church with some of its greatest challenges and most urgent questions. William Henn, OFM Cap, captures this sense when he notes that "the more adequate harmonization of primacy and episcopacy, of the church universal and the local church, is widely considered to be one of the most pressing theological tasks of the Church today."[36]

Finally, while our focus has been on examining the important ways that Vatican I influenced *what* and *how* Vatican II taught on ecclesial authority in *Lumen Gentium* 18–23, it is important to note that the earlier council impacted the style and content of the later one on a much greater scale. Because of its one-sidedness, Vatican I bequeathed to Vatican II unfinished work regarding episcopal authority and the local church. The limitations of Vatican I, however, did not prompt corresponding limitations from Vatican II. Instead, Vatican II's efforts to respond to Vatican I's questions catalyzed an incredibly broad examination of the church and a special concern for the relationship in the church between its universal dimensions and its local dimensions. The elevation of the bishops' role and the rediscovery of the theological significance of the local church prompted by the questions posed by Vatican I meant that the relationship between the pope and the bishops— Rome and the local churches—was not simple in the sense that it was uniform or unidirectional. Determining the relationship

---

[36] See William Henn, "Historical-Theological Synthesis of the Relation between Primacy and Episcopacy during the Second Millennium," in *Il primate del successore de Pietro: Atti del simposio teologico, Roma dicembre 1996* (Vatican City: Libreria Editrice Vaticana, 1997), 219–20.

between these two dimensions would require complex work; it would, however, yield insights that were mutually enriching. Vatican II embraced the work of elucidating the character of local authority but of seeing it in relation to centralized authority. Concern for the relation in the church between its local and universal dimensions became another "special accent" of the council. This accent must be understood as a part of Vatican I's legacy inasmuch as it is developed out of an interest in the episcopacy and the local church that had been occasioned by the council. Thus, we can see that, in a fundamental way, Vatican I impacted *what* and *how* Vatican II taught.

CHAPTER SEVEN

Both Vatican I *and* Vatican II

Go, therefore, and make disciples of all nations, baptizing them in the name of the Father, and of the Son, and of the holy Spirit, teaching them to observe all that I have commanded you. And behold, I am with you always, until the end of the age.

—Matthew 28:19-20

This study has been motivated by a desire to better understand the relationship between Vatican I and Vatican II in order to enhance the church's self-understanding and its ability to speak meaningfully today. Noncontextual readings of these councils have given rise to a sense that their teachings are mutually exclusive and that it is necessary to affirm *either* Vatican I's *or* Vatican II's presentation of the church. The previous chapters have sought to transcend inadequate readings of Vatican I and Vatican II by directing questions of *why*, *how*, and *what* at their texts. Clearer theological and historical contextualization has illumined critical insights regarding the councils' proper interpretations and important aspects of continuity, complementarity, and difference between them. Doing so has allowed their respective voices to be heard more authentically, thereby establishing a perspective from which their teachings and relationship can be viewed with greater precision and overall appreciation.

The effort to cultivate more adequate understandings of Vatican I and Vatican II was undertaken, however, not only in service of advancing these councils' interpretation and clarifying their relationship but also as a means of illuming the character of the church's living tradition. This final chapter will examine how the enhanced appreciation of Vatican I and Vatican II gained in the previous chapters sheds light on this broader reality and, in doing so, contributes to the church's ability to speak meaningfully today. To that end, the chapter considers an approach to harmonizing the teachings of Vatican I and Vatican II that also speaks to the nature of the church's tradition. Articulating a coherent reading of Vatican I and Vatican II does not simply concern the possibility of reconciling particular aspects of the councils' content; it concerns the lenses themselves that are employed in such efforts. In order to make a determination about the proper relationship of Vatican I and Vatican II, we must examine the lenses the councils themselves employ as well as the hermeneutical principles of the tradition of which they are a part.

At the conclusion of his *Models of the Church*, Avery Dulles reflects on the task of harmonization.[1] After describing his five models (later revised to include a sixth), Dulles turns to the question of their relationship. Regarding the compatibility of these models he asks, "Are the differences of horizon mutually exclusive or mutually complementary?"[2] Dulles concludes that holding multiple models in tension with one another is, ultimately, unavoidable given the fact that the church is essentially a mystery and, as such, no model can capture its fullness. In light of this, Dulles asserts that "our method must therefore be to harmonize the models in such a way that their differences become complementary rather than mutually repugnant. . . . In this way it may be possible to gain an understanding of the Church that transcends the limits of any model."[3] Harmonization, as Dulles highlights, depends on identifying a unifying principle that is sufficiently strong to hold disparate elements together in a fruitful tension. Accordingly, judgments about whether Vatican I's and Vatican II's positions can be harmonized involve decisions about the strength of their shared horizon relative to the power of their differences.

---

[1] Avery Dulles, *Models of the Church* (New York: Doubleday, 1974).

[2] Ibid., 179.

[3] Ibid., 185.

As such, evaluations of the compatibility of these two councils are inevitably rooted in views about the proper balance between unity and diversity in the church as well as convictions about what types of unity—and what types of difference—exert the greatest force. Also at stake here are understandings regarding the nature of the Holy Spirit's presence within the church, particularly in its conciliar tradition. A failure to harmonize Vatican I and Vatican II or to identify a unifying hermeneutic raises questions, if not doubts, regarding the guiding presence and animating action of the Spirit in the life of the church. Ultimately, efforts to achieve a greater reconciliation of Vatican I and Vatican II provide a glimpse of theological realities that transcend these two important, yet finite expressions of the church's faith. Thus, our efforts to understand Vatican I's and Vatican II's relationship not only enrich interpretation of these two councils but also enhance a deeper ecclesial self-understanding and self-expression.[4]

I. Looking at the *What, Why,* and *How* of Vatican I and Vatican II

Comparing Vatican I and Vatican II in terms of *why, how,* and *what* the councils taught offers fertile and important ground for achieving a greater reconciliation between their positions. This contextualization reveals the existence of continuity and discontinuity between the councils' texts and allows for a closer examination of these elements by noting the specific location and type of agreement or disagreement. Gaining a more precise understanding of the convergences and divergences between Vatican I and Vatican II is critical. It allows for the kind of careful consideration of the relative weights of their agreements and disagreements that is necessary to make a judgment about their potential harmonization. Comparing Vatican I and Vatican II on particular issues of intent, style, and content establishes a vantage point from which a more informed decision about their relationship can be reached.

---

[4] Pottmeyer, "A New Phase in the Reception of Vatican II," 33.

Central to understanding *why* Vatican I and Vatican II taught what they taught is that each is set in the context of "historical rupture." In his examination of the backdrop of Vatican II, Schloesser describes "historical rupture" as the "definitive passing of an era," a time when the world has to "endure its deepest anxieties."[5] Schloesser's definition establishes a critical context for *why* Vatican II taught as it did. The trauma and existential angst catalyzed by two world wars, the Holocaust, the rise of atheistic communism, and the escalation of the Cold War exercised a significant impact on Vatican II's questions, its methods, and its teachings. John XXIII notes such questions as impetus for his convocation of a council. This critical aspect of *why* the council taught is essential for understanding *what* it taught and *how* it taught. While Schloesser's discussion of "historical rupture" was intended as a hermeneutic tool for approaching Vatican II's documents, there is no doubt that Vatican I also took place at a similar juncture. Shifts in the social, political, economic, and ecclesial spheres in the eighteenth and nineteenth centuries set in motion a series of developments that traumatized the church in profound ways. Vatican I was called in order to discern a response to these changes which, undoubtedly, represented the "passing of an era" and presented challenges which stoked men's and women's "deepest anxieties."[6]

Both Pius IX and John XXIII saw themselves as gathering the bishops at a time when the world stood at a crossroads. Each pope feared that if the church did not respond effectively to the momentous transitions taking place, it might lose its ability to act effectively and carry out its evangelizing mission in the emerging new order. Thus, neither Vatican I nor Vatican II was called to fulfill one of the tasks which had traditionally been the focus of councils: refuting a particular heresy, attending to a specific disciplinary matter, or engaging some aspect of reform; instead, both were called to discern key elements of the church's identity as a means of responding to extraordinary moments in history. Vatican I and Vatican II each sought to preserve the church's voice and demonstrate its ability to speak meaningfully not only on theological

---

[5] Schloesser, "Against Forgetting: Memory, History, Vatican II," 93.
[6] Ibid.

subjects but also to the most urgent questions of its day. This context meant that both councils had to think carefully and broadly about the situation of the world and the presentation of their teachings in ways that their predecessors had not. For *both* Vatican I *and* Vatican II, the backdrop of historical rupture played a critical role in *why* they taught and *what* they taught.

Vatican I and Vatican II are linked, however, not only by the fact that both are set amid epochal shifts but also by the nature of the forces propelling these changes roughly one hundred years apart. Both councils had to engage issues characteristic of what O'Malley has called the "long nineteenth century."[7] According to O'Malley, the long nineteenth century for the Catholic Church "stretches from the French Revolution until the end of the pontificate of Pius XII in 1958. The French Revolution and the philosophy that undergirded it traumatized Catholic officialdom through much of that long century."[8] The Revolution and its effects touched most aspects of Western European culture, and it included rises in secularization and pluralism, an increasingly scientific worldview, and a tendency toward exaggerated individualism. O'Malley captures the attitude well:

> The thinkers of the Enlightenment turned their backs on the past, turned their faces resolutely to the future, and looked forward to ever better things to come. Among those things was a new era of liberty, equality and fraternity. Religion and monarchy would no longer shackle the human spirit. Freedom of expression and freedom of the press were rights that could not be denied. No more religious dogma, for Reason was the only god to be adored. No more hierarchy or privilege by reason of birth. No more kings—or at least no kings without severe constitutional restraints. The list could go on, but progress toward a better future undergirded the mentality. Modernity implied, therefore, a view about historical change.[9]

At the heart of the shifts associated with the long nineteenth century was a new view of change. Modernity, at its core, was fueled by a notion about progress and a desire to move beyond restrictions

---

[7] See O'Malley's discussion of this topic in his chapter, "The Long Nineteenth Century," in O'Malley, *What Happened at Vatican II*, 53–92.

[8] O'Malley, *What Happened at Vatican II*, 4.

[9] Ibid., 54.

that were perceived as "shackling" human freedom. Accordingly the past, with its traditions and esteem for external authority, was eschewed in favor of a world that looked forward and embraced change as a consequence of the autonomy of human reason. These developments forced the church to wrestle with issues such as its role in the public sphere, the nature of ecclesial authority in relation to personal freedom, and the character of legitimate diversity within the unity of the Body of Christ. Perhaps most important, the church had to decide whether it would embrace the modern notion of change or define itself against it.

The questions of the long nineteenth century were at the center of *both* Vatican I *and* Vatican II. To be sure, the specific historical circumstances and the way these issues presented themselves were different in 1869 than in 1962; it remains, however, that many of the most important questions at Vatican I and Vatican II were manifestations of the same intellectual trajectory; fueling this trajectory was the question of change and questions regarding the relationship between the past and the present. John Courtney Murray famously referred to change as "*the* issue under the issues" at Vatican II.[10] Murray's observation captures something fundamental about the council, namely, that each of its documents, in its own way, represents an effort to engage the critical question of how and under what circumstances the church can change. Scholars today have been nearly unanimous in affirming Murray's maxim as an essential hermeneutic for understanding Vatican II. What is less understood is the fact that this topic played a similar role at Vatican I. In many ways, it can be said that the question of change was also "the issue under the issues" in 1869. At its core, Vatican I was concerned with how the church should respond to the advent of liberal ideas and the way they challenged foundational elements of the church's identity such as the validity of revelation, ecclesial authority, and the church's access to truth. Underlying all of its deliberations was an awareness of the need to determine how the church would position itself in regard to

---

[10] John Courtney Murray, "This Matter of Religious Freedom," *America* 112 (January 9, 1965): 43 (emphasis in the original). For an excellent study on Murray, see Barry Hudock, *Struggle Condemnation, Vindication: John Courtney Murray's Journey toward Vatican II* (Collegeville, MN: Liturgical Press, 2015).

these developments. Joseph Burgess points to this reality when he notes, "The First Vatican Council was seen to be concerned with the theology of faith and ecclesiastical certitude. That was not what was believed at the time, not even perhaps by the pope. At the time it was believed to be concerned with the question of questions, whether liberalism and Catholicism could be reconciled." [11] Thus, approximately one hundred years apart, *both* Vatican I *and* Vatican II wrestled with questions regarding how and under what circumstances the church can change as an "issue under the issues" underlying all their deliberations.

A key element of *why* both Vatican I and Vatican II taught as they did was a desire to respond to the spread of modern principles so that their emergence did not eclipse the church's voice. These shared *whys* constitute a fundamental link between the councils and opens up a wider range of interpretive possibility for reconciling them. It is often presumed that *why* Vatican I was called was to define papal infallibility; yet in reality, *why* the council was called was to try to preserve the church's voice amid dramatic changes that threatened to leave it behind. With limited time and a defensive mind-set, it seemed to a majority of bishops that providing a strong view of papal power was the best way of asserting precisely what the world lacked: a reliable principle of authority. Thus, *why* Vatican I taught what it taught was due neither to theological judgments nor an insatiable quest for power in Rome; instead, its goal was to secure for the church a means of self-preservation and self-expression over and against challenges emerging from the long nineteenth century. Similarly, *why* Vatican II taught what it taught was, in large part, to respond to the historical rupture of the mid-twentieth century by updating the church so that it could more effectively demonstrate its ability to make unique and meaningful contributions to contemporary problems. Another key aspect of *why* Vatican II taught what it taught, an element which has generally not been treated in studies of the council's context, is that it sought to bring balance to the unfinished work of its predecessor. The incomplete nature of Vatican I's response to modern developments weakened its teachings both

[11] Burgess, "The Historical Background of Vatican I," 294.

theologically and strategically, rendering it incapable of providing a complete or satisfying response to the major questions of its day. The need for Vatican II to engage many of Vatican I's unanswered questions was not only due to the fact that its predecessor's work was unfinished but also because its limited emphasis on centralized authority seemed out of touch with modern principles and made it difficult for the church to engage the changes and questions of modern society.

In moving from the framing question of *why* to *how*, significant continuities and discontinuities emerge regarding *how* Vatican I and Vatican II responded to the challenges they faced. Both councils looked internally for answers to questions generated externally, and both focused on aspects of the church's nature as a means of engaging transitions taking place in the social and political order. As a result, *both* Vatican I *and* Vatican II can be described as ecclesiological councils. Their focus on the church distinguishes them within the conciliar tradition. Among the twenty-one ecumenical councils in the church's tradition, only these two are typically characterized as councils largely focused on ecclesial questions.[12] This thematic overlap is not a coincidence; in many ways, it connotes a distinct choice by the fathers at Vatican II to embrace the unfinished work of Vatican I. At another level, the council fathers at Vatican II not only adopt Vatican I's questions but also repeat critical aspects of *how* the earlier council treated the issue of ecclesial authority. This repetition affirms both its predecessor's argument and some important aspects of its rationale. A final similarity regarding *how* Vatican I and Vatican II responded to the massive changes of its day is that each council not only turned inward to the nature and mission of the church but also turned outward to the character of the church-world relationship. At both gatherings, the bishops understood one of their central purposes to be demonstrating the way in which the church fit into the new picture of the emerging world. Articulating the church-world relationship

---

[12] Some argue that Trent can also be seen as an ecclesiological council. For some consideration of the strengths and weaknesses of this argument see Bulman and Parrella, *From Trent to Vatican II*, especially John O'Malley's "Trent and Vatican II: Two Styles of Church," 301–19.

was critical to achieving both councils' goals, and this shaped their documents in profound ways.

In other ways, *how* each council responded to its historical and theological situation and the questions of the long nineteenth century differed significantly. In the mind of Pius IX and the majority of bishops at Vatican I, the changes taking place in the world were unambiguously hostile to Christianity and incompatible with its worldview. As such, Pius IX's vision of Vatican I was not that of a council that sought to make a transition with the world but one that would reject the transition the world was making. Vatican I reacted to the developments of its day by distancing itself from the perceived causes of society's struggles and, in turn, highlighting that the church's message and values stood in marked contrast from those of the secular world. This opposition cultivated a fortress mentality whereby the church was presented as possessing all reliable answers and as capable of leading men and women safely through a troubled world. The council's defensive posture was reflected in its style, which favored formulations that were precise, technical, and timeless in character and tone. In constructing its response, Vatican I relied on Christ's promise in Matthew 28:20 ("Behold, I am with you always"): the way it speaks to the constancy of the church, its distinctive elements and the unity of its teachings. Ultimately, *how* Vatican I taught made it clear that it did not seek dialogue or reconciliation but intended to reject most premises of modern development.

Another critical aspect of *how* Vatican I taught is that it contains formulations that are meant to be understood juridically as well as formulations that are meant to be understood theologically. Readers have often misunderstood this double dimension of *how* Vatican I taught because they miss the presence of more than one genre in its texts—the existence of multiple *hows*. While Vatican I's texts include formulations that are intended to be understood in a juridical sense, it is not the case that all of Vatican I's teachings are meant to be understood juridically instead of theologically. Scholarship on papal infallibility and Vatican I all too often lacks a theological framework in general and specific reference to earlier theological reflections on questions concerning the papal office, its primacy and authority, and its place in classic medieval and early modern treatises on the church. At other times, it mistakes moments of juridical definition—which do not reflect theological convictions, *per se*—as theological doctrine so that more is made of passages than should be. Theological readings of the *ex sese* clause, for example, can fall into this category. Vatican I is unique, following in the footsteps of Trent, in that in some ways it reflects the traditional notion that councils were legislative-juridical bodies that issued ordinances, heard cases, and rendered judgments; yet in other ways it sought to move beyond this mold by providing positive theological content.[13] The history of interpreting Vatican I is thus marked with misappropriated theological readings of juridical texts at some points and, at others, the failure to use an adequate historical and theological lens by which to contextualize questions of papal authority.

In turning to *how* Vatican II taught, it is clear that the council charted a different course in its efforts to speak meaningfully in the modern context than its predecessor. John XXIII, like Pius IX, saw the church as poised on the threshold of a new epoch, and he too recognized the potential dangers of modern trends. Rather than adopting a defensive posture that prioritized clarity and emphasized the differences between the church and the world, John XXIII desired a pastoral focus and hoped to highlight common ground between the world's and the church's questions and goals. Thus, upon reaching the crossroads which emerged in the mid-twentieth century, *how* Vatican II reacted was with a greater openness to the world and with efforts to develop a more convincing demonstration of the wisdom of the church's message. Vatican II's response drew direction from Christ's command to "go teach all nations" in Matthew 28:19, which highlights the Gospel's ability to enter all cultures and unite with its authentic elements. As a result, Vatican II's texts are longer, tolerant of greater tension, dialogical in their approach to open questions, and broader in

---

[13] See O'Malley's treatment of this in *What Happened at Vatican II*, particularly in the section titled "Genre, Form Content, Values: 'The Spirit of the Council,'" 44–52.

scope than the texts of previous councils.[14] Thus, the council's more positive view of the world is reflected in not only *what* the council taught but also *how* it taught.

The *how* of Vatican II's teaching makes use of the epideictic rather than the juridical. This shift in genre expressed the bishops' sense that their work was not that of a legislative-juridical body whose purpose is to clarify concepts and outline punishments for transgressions; their work was to hold up the church's wisdom in a way that might inspire others and excite emulation of an ideal.[15] Regarding the council's style, O'Malley notes, "The Council forged almost overnight a new language for conciliar, even theological discourse. That discourse attempted to appeal to affect, to reconcile opposing viewpoints rather than vindicate one of them, and was notably exhortatory, almost homiletical, in style. That style was calculated not so much to judge and legislate as to prepare individuals for a new mind-set with which to approach all aspects of their religious lives."[16] With this language, the council aimed to achieve interior change and conversion rather than observable conformity. It pursued its goals of *aggiornamento* and initiating a dialogue with the world, not only through *what* it taught but also *how* it taught. The juridical approach to ecclesial authority often deployed by Vatican I and the more sacramental approach used by Vatican II mark a distinct discontinuity in *how* each council taught what it taught.

Finally, a consideration of *what* each council taught in regard to ecclesial authority is extremely helpful. In the realm of content, there are clear elements of continuity and discontinuity between Vatican I's and Vatican II's texts. Both councils affirm a strong role for episcopal collegiality as well as papal authority. Additionally, each gathering is explicit that these two authorities are not competitive; rather, they are interdependent and intended to provide

[14] John O'Malley, "Vatican II: Historical Perspectives on Its Uniqueness and Interpretation," in *Vatican II: The Unfinished Agenda; A Look to the Future*, ed. Lucien Richard (New York: Paulist Press, 1988), 22–32.

[15] O'Malley, *What Happened at Vatican II*, 47.

[16] O'Malley, "Vatican II: Historical Perspectives on Its Uniqueness and Interpretation," 27.

mutual support. After making such affirmations, however, neither council works out the precise relationship between the two. In considering *what* Vatican I teaches, it teaches that Christ's promise to remain in the church (Matt 28:20) includes the guarantee that the Roman pontiff is able to teach without error in certain circumstances. This strong view is tempered by limits and silences, and it reflects efforts to contextualize its view of papal power within a larger horizon. Because of the council's premature suspension and other intervening factors, however, Vatican I's treatment of the papacy is not properly contextualized within a more comprehensive vision of the church, and it can seem, on a quick reading, to neglect the authority of the episcopate. Shifting to *what* Vatican II taught, the council offers a robust articulation of episcopal collegiality that gives strong support for diverse expressions of the Gospel. It teaches that the origin of the bishops' authority is sacramental and collegial. Affirming that bishops have responsibility for the whole church, *Lumen Gentium* also argues that, as part of the episcopal college, they are subjects of supreme authority in the church. While Vatican II's treatment of local authority affirms Vatican I's position on centralized authority, its disinterest in integrating the two leads some to the conclusion that its "new" content regarding the episcopacy is what is primarily important. Thus, even as Vatican II teaches on matters of papal and episcopal authority, its silences leave space for continued reflection and development on their interrelation.

The relationship between episcopal and papal authority is at the heart of *both* Vatican I *and* Vatican II. While each council has this relationship at the forefront of its deliberations, neither provides a satisfying description of it. Questions regarding the relationship between the "center and periphery" in the church were so important and pervasive at Vatican II that O'Malley has identified this theme, like change, as one of the "issues under the issues" at the council.[17] Scholars have celebrated O'Malley's insight as a

---

[17] Specifically, O'Malley describes this "issue" as "the relationship in the church of center to periphery, or, put more concretely, how authority is properly distributed between the papacy, including the Congregations (departments or bureaus) of the Vatican Curia, and the rest of the church." O'Malley, *What Happened at Vatican II*, 8.

significant advance in understanding Vatican II's theology as a whole. While O'Malley asserts the center-periphery question as central to Vatican II, it was without question a dominant force at Vatican I as well. It is the center-periphery question which is, in fact, the central topic in the debate between the minority bishops and the majority bishops and which occupies, for example, Gasser's efforts to properly position *Pastor Aeternus* prior to its final vote. It is precisely the desire to achieve a more authentic balance between center and periphery that the minority hoped to preserve, through the inclusion of key limits and silences within *Pastor Aeternus* and in their efforts after the council to keep its unfinished status alive. Ultimately, *both* Vatican I *and* Vatican II, in fundamental ways, wrestled with the relationship in the church between the center and the periphery, and for both councils this question was a primary lens through which they engaged their work.

While a focus on the question of change unites the two councils, *what* Vatican I and Vatican II taught on this topic represents a difference between them. Vatican I resisted the view of change associated with the long nineteenth century, instead preferring a notion that truth is certain and unchangeable in every time and place. In its defensive posture, the church wanted to emphasize that not everything is subject to endless and unpredictable change; rather, truth is timeless and immune from corruption. Vatican II also engaged the question of change, but it generally offered a different response than its predecessor. The council upheld the importance of immutability in the church, but it did not see all things in the church as immutable. It affirmed the need for development and the fact that the existence of diverse expressions of the Good News corresponds to the nature of the truth it reveals. This recognition was powerfully expressed in Pope John XXIII's observation in Vatican II's opening address: "The substance of the ancient doctrine of the Deposit of Faith is one thing, and the way in which it is presented is another."[18] Vatican II's affirmation does not mean that the basic truths of the faith change. Instead, it highlights the reality that believers come to deeper insights concerning

---

[18] John XXIII, "*Gaudet mater ecclesia*," in Anderson, *Council Daybook Vatican II*, 1:25–29, at 27.

those truths and the way that these truths illuminate and are illuminated by contemporary conditions. These different views regarding the possibility and potential benefit of change are often used as evidence of the fundamental incompatibility of the councils' positions.

Looking at questions of *what*, *why*, and *how* Vatican I and Vatican II taught and comparing the two councils from this perspective highlights the existence of both real unity and real difference between them. In light of these clear elements of continuity and discontinuity between these councils, the question that remains is: can their positions be harmonized? As we will see, to a great extent, Vatican I and Vatican II illumine the answer to this question through their own texts.

II. Matthew 28:19-20

A critical lens for understanding the inherent complementarity of Vatican I's and Vatican II's positions is found in the councils' respective usages of two scriptural passages: Matthew 28:19 and 28:20. The unity amid diversity of these passages provides a way of understanding how Vatican I's and Vatican II's texts may be harmonized. In presenting its view of papal authority, Vatican I roots its position in the promise given to Christ at the conclusion of Matthew's Gospel: "And behold, I am with you always until the end of the age" (Matt 28:20). *Aeterni Patris* and *Pastor Aeternus* employ Christ's pledge to remain in the church and guide it as evidence for the claim that the church is capable of teaching reliably and offering stability amid the uncertainty of the world. This reliance in Vatican I's texts on the last line of Matthew's Gospel becomes particularly noteworthy in light of John XXIII's characterization of Vatican II's aims nearly one hundred years later. In a historic radio address on September 12, 1962, John XXIII was asked to characterize the work of the upcoming council.[19] Speaking to an international audience, Pope John described the bishops'

---

[19] "Pope's Address to the World Month before the Council Opened," in *Council Daybook Vatican II*, 1:18–20, at 19.

task as a continuation of the command which the Lord gave at the end of Matthew's Gospel when he said, "Go, therefore, and make disciples of all nations; baptizing them in the name of the Father, and of the Son, and of the Holy Spirit, teaching them to observe all that I have commanded you" (Matt 28:19). Pope John's use of the penultimate line of Matthew's Gospel was intended to highlight the *ad intra* and *ad extra* dimensions of the council's work; its connection with the theological foundation of Vatican I, however, cannot be ignored. The fact that Vatican I and Vatican II both root their theologies in two successive lines from Matthew's Gospel—and not only successive passages but also interdependent passages—provides critical insight into the nature of the relationship between them.

The promise and mission Christ gives his disciples in Matthew 28:19 and 28:20 are inseparable. Without the assurance that their efforts would be safeguarded from error by the guarantee of Christ's constant guidance, the disciples would lack the courage to go out and proclaim the Good News. It is the pledge of Christ's perpetual presence (Matt 28:20) which instills in them the confidence to move outward and preach the Gospel throughout the nations (Matt 28:19). Yet, the relationship between Christ's promise and his commission does not flow in one direction; it is also the case that the experience of going out and meeting Christ anew in "all nations" (Matt 28:19) allows the disciples to know Christ's presence among them more deeply (Matt 28:20). Together, Matthew 28:19 and 28:20 represent integral and integrating dimensions of the church's life: knowledge of God's word and the impulse to proclaim it. These aspects comprise the upward spiral of the church's mission in that Christians must know the content of the Good News if they are to communicate it effectively; yet they cannot truly know the substance of this message apart from engaging the world. *Both* preserving a faithful representation of the ancient faith *and* proclaiming it in an intelligible and compelling manner within a particular context constitute inseparable aspects within the one goal of spreading the Good News to all the ends of the earth.

Like Mathew 28:19 and 28:20, Vatican I and Vatican II can be seen as conveying distinct but interdependent elements of the church, elements that are often seen as competitive but are, on the contrary, mutually edifying. Ultimately, Vatican I and Vatican II share the same fundamental goal of evangelization; both seek to find new and effective ways of proclaiming the Gospel in a particular time and place. Within that broader framework, the two councils are united on an even more particular level by their common effort to demonstrate the ongoing relevance of the church's voice amid the rise of modern developments which threatened to leave it behind. Each strives to show that the church is capable of speaking meaningfully to the urgent questions of its day by focusing on a particular *ad intra* dimension of the church's life. Working from a hermeneutic of conciliar reception, one can interpret their presentations of the church as contributions to an ongoing reflection of the church's own identity rather than as innovative or oppositional models of church or ecclesial authority. Further, we have adduced clear evidence that Vatican II expressly saw one of its main tasks as maintaining continuity with its predecessor and completing its work. There is explicit complementarity between the two councils' teachings which is made possible by Vatican I's deliberate restraint and Vatican II's attention to Vatican I's silences. It is the case that Vatican I and Vatican II can rely on the concluding lines of Matthew's Gospel because, on a fundamental level, they share common questions and aims.

The strength of this shared horizon unites Vatican I and Vatican II in a way that allows the real differences between them to be seen as complementary rather than mutually exclusive. The councils' common intent, common foundation in the church's tradition, and complementary teachings connect them in profound ways which are able to hold their differences in noncontradictory tension. The fact that Vatican I treated the pope's authority and Vatican II focused on episcopal authority should not be seen as polarizing the councils but as uniting them in the common aim of responding meaningfully to questions of authority that became unavoidable in the course of the long nineteenth century. Vatican I's efforts to preserve the church's voice were rooted in its desire to provide the clarity and stability which it sensed that the world lacked and people craved. Vatican II also attempted to integrate its voice into the contemporary conversation, but its method was one of identifying common questions, shared concerns, and an ability to meaningfully contribute to contemporary conversations regarding urgent situations. Seen within the larger framework of evangelizing the modern world, the distinct elements of these two councils can be seen as complementary not competitive efforts. From this perspective, we can see that *both* Vatican I's concern for clarity and precision *and* Vatican II's focus on mystery and dialogue play key roles in the life of the church. *Both* Vatican II's sense that the church is a partner with the world *and* Vatican I's sense that the church is a prophet which must critique the world are aspects of the church's identity. The church needs to stress *both* the constancy and the eternal character of God's revelation *and* the fact that expressions of truth develop over time and adapt to particular circumstances.

Presenting Vatican I's and Vatican II's formulations as an *either/ or* choice between consistency or plurality, precise teaching or openness, and distinctiveness from the world or commonality with it can seem like an easy or obvious set of contrasts. A consequence of such juxtapositions, however, is the suggestion that the Christian tradition does not work as a whole. It calls into question the belief that the same Holy Spirit guides the church in all times and gives rise to a sense that the church's own teachings cannot be reconciled. It suggests that differences in the way that the councils approach ecclesial authority or the existence of differences in their form or content are sufficient to undermine the fundamental unity between them. Such a rigid view of what constitutes authentic agreement conveys a sense of catholicity as uniformity and a rigidity that is incapable of embracing the fullness of God's revelation. Put another way, arguments that assert that Vatican I and Vatican II are mutually exclusive are operating with a lens that is insufficiently dynamic to account for the mystery and totality of creation. It is a hermeneutic which not only fails the councils but also, more important, approaches doctrine as inflexible and isolated from interpretive development. If differences within and between conciliar decrees, or between councils, are too hastily reconciled, then elements of the mystery they seek to express will be lost. The isolation of Vatican I and the presumption that Vatican I and Vatican II are mutually exclusive are examples of instances where the church has been impoverished by an inability to live with tensions inherent to its nature.

The fact that *both* Vatican I *and* Vatican II offer distinct but complementary presentations of the church illumines the dynamic nature of the church's catholicity. It demonstrates the way that the church's living tradition is capable of holding dogmatic tension together within an even more profound unity. In holding Vatican I's and Vatican II's teachings together in a fruitful tension, we have the opportunity to glimpse beyond the councils to the way that the church's catholicity is not constituted by geographic extension or a monotonous repetition of sameness. It instead consists in the ability to incorporate all aspects of legitimate diversity within the oneness of the Christian message. To speak meaningfully in the modern world, the church must be able to account for the diversity which characterizes it, including that which is found in its dogmatic tradition. Christians cannot communicate how the plurality of human experience is synthesized within the unity of God's word if they do not understand the character of that unity and its foundation. Similarly, Christians cannot understand the nature and force of the church's unity apart from seeing the diversity which authentically flows from and expresses it. The real and significant differences between Vatican I and Vatican II do not negate the reality that they both illumine the oneness of God's revelation. In fact, these differences highlight the way that the tradition of the church's councils is characterized by continuous unity amid diverse conciliar expressions.

Catholicity as unity in diversity does not imply that no real differences exist within the church, nor does it suggest that discontinuity disappears or becomes insignificant in the presence of continuity; on the contrary, it means that legitimate diversity is necessary for vibrant unity. Articulating this unity allows us to see how Vatican I's and Vatican II's respective teachings on matters such as authority and freedom may be seen as complementary rather than as incoherent. Further, the work of harmonizing Vatican I and Vatican II under a hermeneutic of unity-continuity does not mean that their teachings should be equally emphasized. Vatican II provides a much more comprehensive and adequate articulation of the nature of the church. Vatican I's teaching is far more limited on a variety of levels. So asserting that *both* Vatican I *and* Vatican II are necessary and legitimate expressions of the church does not mean that they are equally adequate. Put succinctly, saying *both/and* does not mean 50/50—it means that the two councils must be held in appropriate tension.

A properly contextualized reading shows that Vatican I's emphasis on centralized, papal authority need not be seen as competitive with Vatican II's vigorous support of episcopal authority. In fact, the two depend on one another. The dynamic plurality and diverse local expressions held up in Vatican II require a robust unity to hold them together. In the absence of a unifying principle, real diversity easily breaks apart. The converse is also true. In the absence of meaningful diversity, unity easily becomes static and seems incapable of integrating many distinct experiences, much less all of reality. Therefore, erring too much on the side of the papal and centralized authority risks eclipsing a vibrant diversity that witnesses to the Gospel's ability to integrate all authentic reality within the oneness of its revelation. Similarly, erring on localized authority and collegiality without adequate concern for unity risks atomization. Ultimately, the differences between Vatican I and Vatican II show that, within the mystery of the church, unity and diversity often work in a direct relationship. A strong papacy is not realized in a weak episcopacy nor in the repetition of endless sameness; rather, the strength of the center is truly realized only in its ability to hold dynamic diversity together and integrate all authentic reality within the oneness of the Gospel. A strong episcopate is not achieved in a weak papacy; rather, it depends on a unity compelling enough to hold real difference together. In this way, the existence of real and meaningful differences between Vatican I and Vatican II attests to the true dynamism of the church's living tradition.

III. An Ongoing Conversation

Achieving a greater reconciliation of Vatican I and Vatican II sheds light on many of the developments taking place in the church today. In the years since Vatican II, the church has seen attention shift to questions of reception. Prior to Vatican II, this locus did not demand a great deal of theological attention. In fact, before the council, reception was generally not considered a properly theological concern; instead it was viewed as a minor matter of housekeeping wherein it was decided how truths elucidated at the center could be conveyed to the rest of the church. In such frameworks, reception was seen as a passive process, one which Yves Congar said could be characterized as a form of "submission."[20] Jean-Marie Tillard noted that the retrieval of reception as a robust theological category stands as "one of the most important theological re-discoveries of our century."[21] By turning to the issue of reception, the church, after Vatican II, directed its attention to questions of how local communities participate in establishing structures of belief and practice. It shifted to seeing reception as a dynamic process of communication whereby the magisterium and the rest of the faithful seek to develop increasingly rich expressions of what God has revealed and how it is held by the community's lived faith.[22] As such, reception has come to be recognized as more than an administrative task. It connotes an important theological issue rooted in ecclesiological commitments, specifically, convictions regarding how authority is conceived and exercised in the church.

The "rediscovery" of reception speaks to the importance and the character of Vatican I's and Vatican II's relationship. Much has been made in this volume about the fact that Vatican I was unable to complete its entire program of work. As was seen in chapter 4, the debate over whether the council was finished or unfinished played a key role in the early reception of its texts. For the minority bishops at Vatican I, the council's prorogued status meant that

---

[20] Yves Congar, in his influential article "Reception as an Ecclesiological Reality," commented on the absence of a theological consideration of reception prior to Vatican II by noting that "the question of reception was all but eliminated when the ecclesiology of communion was substituted by a pyramidal theory of the Church: a mass determined and activated by its peak, in which and from which and for which the Holy Spirit is considered as scarcely little more than the guarantor of the Church's hierarchy." See Yves Congar, "La réception comme réalité écclesiologique," in *Revue des Sciences Philosophiques et Théologiques* 56 (1972): 369–403. Published in English as "Reception as an Ecclesial Reality," in *Election and Consensus in the Church*, ed. G. Alberigo and A. Weiler (New York: Herder and Herder, 1972).

[21] Ormond Rush, *Still Interpreting Vatican II* (New York: Paulist Press, 2004), 53.

[22] Wolfgang Beinert, "The Subjects of Ecclesial Reception," *The Jurist* 57 (1997): 321–30.

its teachings could not be fully understood because they lacked the context the council fathers intended. The maximalist bishops advanced a view that Vatican I was finished and that the points the council had not been able to treat were rendered moot, given what it had been able to accomplish. What eventually became clear to both sides was that the questions left unanswered by Vatican I did not fade away; instead, they gained even greater urgency. This urgency became especially apparent when Vatican II was called and the council fathers chose to place many of these questions at the center of the council's deliberations. Yet, like Vatican I, Vatican II *was also unable to complete its work*. The "unfinished" character of Vatican II has played an increasingly large role in debates over the council's interpretation.[23] Interestingly, the inverse of what transpired in Vatican I's reception has followed after Vatican II; specifically, a majority of interpreters now argue that the council is unfinished, while a minority argues that its work is, in fact, complete. In a pattern similar to that seen in Vatican I, the issues left unresolved in 1965 have reemerged in the discussions that came after Vatican II, in this case, in conversations about the nature of reception.

Debates over reception are an extension of the church's ongoing struggle to present an identity consistent with the deposit of faith while also providing meaningful expressions of its message to diverse people who face complex, modern problems. As such, they can be seen as representing an extension of Vatican II's consideration of local authority and its efforts to reach a greater synthesis of the church's universal and local dimensions. Current conversations about reception, however, also ought to be seen as engaging Vatican I's unfinished questions in that they concern efforts to understand the character of universal authority and its relation to other types of authority in the church. In this way, the advent of attention on the issue of reception can be seen as *an effort to continue conversations begun at Vatican I and continued at Vatican II*. At the heart of disagreements about reception lie many of the same questions that dominated Vatican I and Vatican II, questions regarding

[23] See Kristin Colberg, "The Hermeneutics of Vatican II: Reception, Authority and the Debate over the Council's Interpretation," *Horizons* 38, no. 2 (2011): 230–52.

authority, freedom, and how universal and local authorities co-operate in the development of ecclesial teachings. In many ways, it is the same "issues under the issues"—change and the relation in the church between the center and the periphery—which are at the heart of contemporary conversations about reception. Achieving a greater reconciliation of Vatican I with Vatican II therefore promotes a more nuanced appreciation of developments in the church which followed both councils, especially the rise of recent debates over the issue of reception. Such an understanding clarifies how these discussions and changing structures in the church today are not random developments or unrelated to what preceded them. They are deeply connected to the common questions at the heart of these two councils.

The emergence of questions of reception affirms the existence of a story and important relationship between Vatican I and Vatican II. The fact that reception has surfaced as a central theological concern demonstrates that Vatican I was not overcome by Vatican II in a competitive sense. If Vatican II's articulation of a strong sense of episcopal power was taken as the definitive word on ecclesiastical authority, there would be no need to balance it with the centralized view of authority advanced at Vatican I. Additionally, if it were the case that only elements of difference could be recognized between these two councils, and, as such, they could only be viewed as mutually exclusive, then articulating a view of authority and a mode of reception would merely be a matter of choosing between them. Identifying a trajectory of questions that begins with Vatican I, continues through Vatican II, and is manifest in discussions of reception and the reshaping of the church today offers evidence of a dynamic relationship between the two councils and the necessity of achieving a higher level of reconciliation between them.

IV. Conclusion

Vatican I and Vatican II are linked by more than just geography. Inadequate, noncontextual interpretations have led some to the conclusion that these councils are mutually exclusive and that the only connection between them is their setting in St. Peter's Basilica. This assumption proceeds from a false and dangerous dichotomy. Choosing *either* Vatican I *or* Vatican II is unnecessary because *both* Vatican I's *and* Vatican II's presentations of the church are authentic and interrelated representations of the Christian faith. Insisting on a choice between *either* Vatican I *or* Vatican II is also perilous because it contradicts the church's own hermeneutic principles while calling into question its fundamental conviction about the presence of the Holy Spirit guiding the church.

For some, the coherence and compatibility of Vatican I and Vatican II seem frustrated because their positions on papal authority and collegiality are not fully reconciled. The realities that both councils seek to express, however, establish that Christian coherence is not achieved in precision and full clarity but in dynamism. Choosing *either* Vatican I *or* Vatican II does not clarify the truth of the church's nature and mission; only holding all the aspects in tension with one another can accomplish that. The fact that Vatican I's and Vatican II's positions have not yet been fully synthesized is not a failure. On the contrary, the reality that the church seeks to communicate is a reality that cannot be circumscribed. An active and ongoing reception of conciliar teachings is indicative of the way that Christian teachings are not merely stacked one on top of the other but are, instead, integrated together into the life of the faithful through the spirit of Christ who makes all things new. The church ought not move too quickly to resolve this struggle, because this tension is inherent to its very nature and mission. Instead, the ecclesial community must learn to embrace the tension that necessarily characterizes its efforts to express key elements of its identity.

Christians today hope for a church that can speak meaningfully to their most urgent questions. They also hope for a church that can sustain a vibrant yet coherent diversity while witnessing to the fundamental truths of the Christian faith. This hope is fulfilled, in part, through a properly conceived view of the relationship between Vatican I and Vatican II. A dynamic understanding of the relationship between these councils demonstrates a confidence that God is leading God's people to increasingly deeper understandings of the mystery of Christian faith. Affirming that both

Vatican I and Vatican II offer complementary views of the church, therefore, is not merely about reconciling their particular teachings; it is a witness to God leading men and women toward God's promises. Recognizing a dynamic relationship between Vatican I and Vatican II brings confidence, not simply because the church's teachings can be seen as coherent but also because their complementarity indicates that the church's teachings reflect the faith of the community and speak to its experiences and most urgent questions. Arriving at a proper understanding of the relationship between Vatican I and Vatican II, therefore, initiates a new phase of ecclesial self-understanding and self-expression, enhancing the church's ability to "go teach all nations."

Index